HOME EXTENDED

KÖNEMANN

© 2018 koenemann.com GmbH
www.koenemann.com

**ÉDITIONS
PLACE DES
VICTOIRES**

© 2018 Éditions Place des Victoires
6, rue du Mail – 75002 Paris,
pour la présente édition.
www.victoires.com
Dépôt légal : 3ᵉ trimestre 2018
ISBN : 978-2-8099-1560-0

Editorial coordinator: Claudia Martínez Alonso
Art director: Mireia Casanovas Soley
Editor and texts: Francesc Zamora Mola
Layout: Cristina Simó Perales
Translation: Thinking Abroad

Printed in China by Shenzhen Hua Xin Colour-printing & Platemaking Co., Ltd

ISBN 978-3-7419-2136-0

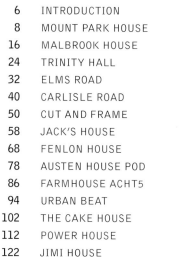

Introduction by **Paul Archer, architect director at Paul Archer Design**

When much of our existing housing stock was built, lifestyles were very different. This has meant that a large proportion of architect's work has been adapting these older buildings, rather than building afresh. We have needed to develop new skills.

We all understand that we don't live like Victorians any more, but in reality, we don't live like we did even twenty-five years ago. Our families are different, our social norms have changed, and amongst many other changes, we use technology in ways unimagined just a generation ago. The challenge is thus to adapt our old buildings to our new ways of living, whilst not destroying what we like about the older houses.

Adaption will often mean adding more space. This will often be to the back, the roof or the side, or even sometimes underneath, whilst retaining the original building's front as part of the streetscape. But it can also mean radical changes to the way the interiors are organized. Most older buildings are very cellular, reflecting the available building technology and social conventions at the time. But we like to live in much more open and airy spaces, and new structural materials and building methods make it straightforward to remove walls and free the space.

One approach to this is to simply continue and copy the style and character of the original building, so there is little difference between old and new. But there is a braver approach. We can build our extensions to today's standards, and use our creativity and imagination to create new and exciting residential architecture. This can have a hugely positive impact on our quality of life.

Modern designers have a whole new world of materials and technologies at hand to build our new homes. Glass technology has transformed what we can do with daylight. Its thermal performance has improved so much that we can enjoy large expanses, connecting inside and outside, without heat gain or loss. The introduction of the steel frame into domestic architecture has meant it is easy to make large open spaces. This open plan has been embraced as the preferred family space, with room for cooking, dining and socializing, all in the same area.

New and old can be happily married together by the architect, who should be able to design an extension that complements the original house without slavishly copying the original style. This can be done in many ways, and is what makes the task creatively interesting. Sometimes it can be the proportions of the old house that guide the design — like dividing new glass doors in the same rhythm as the original windows. Or it can be the materials — like using slate vertical cladding on the new walls when there's slate tiles on the old roof.

This book is about the challenge of adapting our old buildings to our new lifestyles in lots of different and creative ways. Old buildings have proved themselves flexible to changing necessities, and are key to the regeneration of our built environment. We can all benefit from the best of both worlds, new and old together. Not by pastiche, but by confident modern design.

Als ein Großteil der heute bestehenden Häuser gebaut wurde, waren die Lebensstile ganz andere. Das bedeutet, dass ein großer Teil der Arbeit von Architekten in der Anpassung dieser älteren Gebäude besteht, statt im Bau neuer Häuser. Dazu mussten wir neue Fähigkeiten entwickeln und Kompetenzen erwerben. Natürlich ist uns allen klar, dass wir nicht mehr wie im Viktorianischen Zeitalter leben, doch tatsächlich leben wir nicht einmal mehr so wie noch vor fünfundzwanzig Jahren. Unsere Familien sind anders, unsere gesellschaftlichen Normen haben sich gewandelt und neben vielen anderen Veränderungen nutzen wir heute Technologien auf eine Art, die nur eine Generation zuvor noch unvorstellbar war. Die Herausforderung besteht also darin, unsere alten Gebäude an unsere neue Lebensweise anzupassen und dabei das zu erhalten, was wir an den alten Häusern mögen.

Die Anpassung bringt häufig die Schaffung von mehr Raum mit sich. Dies geschieht oft auf der Rückseite, im Dach oder an der Seite, manchmal sogar unter bestehenden Gebäuden, während die originale Fassade als Teil des Straßenbildes erhalten wird. Doch sie kann auch radikale Veränderungen an der Art, wie Innenräume angelegt sind, bedeuten. Die meisten älteren Gebäude sind sehr zellulär, sie spiegeln die verfügbaren Bautechniken und die sozialen Konventionen ihrer Entstehungszeit wider. Doch leben wir heute gern in viel offeneren und luftigeren Räumen und neue Baumaterialien und -methoden machen es leicht, Wände zu entfernen und Räume zu erweitern.

Eine mögliche Herangehensweise ist hier einfach die Fortsetzung und Kopie von Stil und Charakter des ursprünglichen Gebäudes, sodass der Unterschied zwischen Alt und Neu gering ist. Doch es gibt einen mutigeren Ansatz. Wir können unsere Erweiterungen nach heutigen Standards bauen und unsere Kreativität und Phantasie spielen lassen, um neue und aufregende Wohnarchitektur zu schaffen. Dies kann eine enorm positive Wirkung auf unsere Lebensqualität haben.

Modernen Designern steht eine ganze neue Welt an Materialien und Technologien zur Verfügung, um unsere neuen Häuser zu bauen. Die Glastechnologie hat die Möglichkeiten, mit Tageslicht zu arbeiten, transformiert. Die thermischen Eigenschaften von Glas haben sich so stark verbessert, dass wir uns großer Flächen erfreuen können, die Innen und Außen miteinander verbinden, ohne Wärmezufuhr oder -verlust zu erleiden. Die Einführung des Stahlrahmens in die Wohngebäudearchitektur hat dazu geführt, dass es heutzutage leicht ist, große offene Räume zu schaffen. Diese durchgehende, offene Raumgestaltung ist als bevorzugter Familienraum angenommen worden, mit Platz zum Kochen, Essen und Zusammensein, alles in einem Raum.

Neu und Alt können durch den Architekten glücklich vereint werden, der in der Lage sein sollte, eine Erweiterung zu entwerfen, die das ursprüngliche Gebäude ergänzt, ohne den Originalstil sklavisch zu imitieren. Dies kann auf vielerlei Art erreicht werden und es ist das, was die Aufgabe kreativ anspruchsvoll und interessant macht. Manchmal können es die Proportionen des alten Hauses sein, die den Entwurf leiten – wie die Aufteilung von neuen Glastüren im selben Rhythmus wie die Originalfenster. Oder es können die Materialien sein – wie die vertikale Verwendung von Schiefer an den neuen Wänden, wenn das alte Dach mit Schiefer gedeckt ist.

In diesem Buch geht es um die Herausforderung, unsere alten Gebäude auf unterschiedlichste und kreative Art an unsere neuen Lebensstile anzupassen. Alte Gebäude haben sich als flexibel gegenüber Wandlungsbedarf erwiesen und sind für die Regeneration unserer alten baulichen Umgebung ausschlaggebend. Wir können alle vom Besten aus beidem profitieren, dem Neuen und dem Alten zusammen. Nicht durch Persiflage, sondern durch selbstbewusstes modernes Design.

Lorsque la plupart des maisons existant aujourd'hui ont été construites, les styles de vie étaient bien différents. Ainsi une grande partie du travail des architectes consiste à adapter ces vieux bâtiments plutôt que d'en construire de nouveaux. Il nous a fallu développer de nouvelles compétences.

Nous sommes tous bien conscients que nous ne vivons plus comme à l'ère victorienne, mais en réalité nous ne vivons déjà plus comme il y a encore vingt-cinq ans. La structure familiale a changé, nos normes sociales ont évolué, et parmi de nombreux autres changements, notre utilisation de la technologie est telle qu'elle aurait été inimaginable il y a à peine une génération. Le défi consiste donc à adapter nos anciennes structures à nos nouvelles façons de vivre, tout en évitant de détruire ce que nous aimons dans ces maisons d'une autre époque.

Adapter est souvent synonyme de créer davantage d'espace. Il sera souvent ajouté sur l'arrière, sur le toit ou sur les côtés, ou même parfois au-dessous d'un bâtiment, tout en en conservant la façade originale dans son contexte urbain. Mais cela peut signifier des changements radicaux dans la façon dont les intérieurs sont agencés. La plupart des maisons anciennes sont très cellulaires, ce qui reflète la technologie du bâtiment et les conventions sociales en vigueur à l'époque. Mais nous aimons vivre dans des espaces bien plus ouverts et aérés, et de nouveaux matériaux et systèmes de construction facilitent l'élimination des murs et la libération de l'espace.

L'une des approches consiste à prolonger tout simplement le style et le caractère du bâtiment d'origine et à le copier, de sorte qu'il y ait peu de différence entre l'ancien et le nouveau. Mais il existe une approche plus audacieuse. Nous pouvons contruire nos extensions en suivant les normes actuelles, et utiliser notre créativité et notre imagination pour bâtir une architecture résidentielle novatrice et palpitante. Cela peut avoir un impact extrêmement positif sur notre qualité de vie.

Les designers modernes disposent de toute une nouvelle gamme de matériaux et de technologies pour construire nos nouvelles maisons. La technologie du verre a transformé ce qu'il est possible de faire avec la lumière du jour. Ses performances thermiques se sont améliorées au point que l'on peut profiter de vastes surfaces vitrées, connexion entre intérieur et extérieur, sans gain ni perte de chaleur. Grâce à l'introduction de la structure métallique dans l'architecture domestique, il est devenu plus facile de créer de larges espaces ouverts. Cette « pièce ouverte » est devenue l'espace familial privilégié, procurant de la place pour cuisiner, organiser des dîners et des réceptions, le tout dans la même pièce.

L'ancien et le nouveau peuvent être conjugués harmonieusement par l'architecte, qui devrait être à même de concevoir une extension qui complète la maison d'origine sans en reproduire servilement le style. Cela peut se faire de diverses manières, et la tâche en est d'autant plus intéressante au niveau créatif. Parfois le design peut être guidé par les proportions de l'ancienne maison – comme lorsque la division de nouvelles portes vitrées reproduit le rythme des fenêtres d'origine. Ou bien il peut s'agir des matériaux utilisés – comme le fait de poser un bardage vertical en ardoise sur les nouveaux murs pour rappeler la couverture en ardoise de l'ancien toit.

Ce livre traite du challenge que constitue l'adaptation de nos anciens bâtiments à nos nouveaux styles de vie de toutes sortes de façons différentes et créatives. Les vieilles maisons se sont montrées souples face aux nécessités de changement, et sont primordiales pour la régénération de notre environnement bâti. Nous pouvons tous jouir du meilleur de ces deux mondes, la conjugaison de l'ancien et du nouveau. Non pas par le biais du pastiche, mais au moyen d'un design moderne affirmé.

Cuando la mayor parte de las viviendas existentes se construyeron, el estilo de vida de las familias que las habitaban era muy distinto. Una parte muy importante del trabajo arquitectónico ha sido adaptar estos edificios a los nuevos tiempos para no construirlos de nuevo. Y este tipo de trabajo ha implicado el desarrollo de nuevas habilidades.

Todos somos muy conscientes de que ya no vivimos como en la época victoriana. Sin embargo, la realidad es que nuestra forma de vida es diferente de la de hace veinticinco años. La estructura familiar ha cambiado, las normas sociales han evolucionado y, entre otros muchos cambios, usamos la tecnología de forma inimaginable para la generación anterior. El reto es por ello adaptar nuestros antiguos edificios a nuestra forma moderna de vivir, sin destruir lo que apreciamos de estas viviendas.

Y la adaptación ha significado, en muchas ocasiones, añadir más espacio. Muchas veces en la parte de atrás, en un lateral o en el tejado, e incluso por debajo, para mantener intacta la fachada principal del edificio como parte del paisaje urbanístico. Pero también puede implicar un cambio radical en la forma de organizar el interior de la vivienda. La mayoría de los edificios antiguos están muy compartimentados, reflejando la tecnología de construcción disponible en su época y las convenciones sociales del momento. Pero hoy en día preferimos vivir en espacios abiertos y amplios. Gracias a los nuevos materiales estructurales y los métodos de construcción actuales se pueden eliminar paredes y liberar el espacio.

Para esta adaptación podemos continuar y copiar el estilo y carácter del edificio original, de forma que haya poca diferencia entre lo antiguo y lo nuevo. Pero hay una visión más atrevida. Podemos crear las extensiones siguiendo los estándares actuales y usar nuestra creatividad e imaginación para construir una arquitectura residencial nueva y vibrante. Este enfoque puede tener un impacto muy positivo en nuestra calidad de vida.

Los diseñadores modernos tienen a su alcance un nuevo mundo de materiales y tecnologías para la construcción de nuevos hogares. La tecnología del vidrio ha transformado lo que podemos hacer con la luz natural. Su eficiencia térmica ha mejorado tanto que podemos disfrutar de grandes superficies de cristal que conectan interior y exterior sin perder o ganar calor. La introducción de los perfiles de acero en la arquitectura residencial ha facilitado conseguir grandes espacios abiertos. Esta zona abierta se ha convertido en el espacio preferido de la familia: un lugar para cocinar, comer y socializar, todo en el mismo lugar.

El arquitecto puede unir armoniosamente lo nuevo y lo viejo. Puede diseñar una extensión que complemente la casa existente, sin copiar servilmente el estilo original. Puede hacerse de muchas formas distintas, lo que hace que el trabajo sea muy interesante desde el punto de vista creativo. A veces el diseño se guía por las proporciones de la casa original, y se dividen las nuevas puertas de cristal siguiendo el patrón de las ventanas originales. O por los materiales, usando un revestimiento en pizarra en las nuevas paredes, si se usó este material en el tejado de la vivienda original.

Este libro trata el reto de adaptar nuestros antiguos edificios a nuestra nueva forma de vida, de muchas formas distintas y muy creativas. Los edificios originales se han mostrado flexibles al cambio de necesidades y claves para la regeneración de nuestro entorno. Todos nos podemos beneficiar de lo mejor de ambos mundos, lo antiguo y lo nuevo juntos. Y sin ser un pastiche, sino mostrando un diseño moderno lleno de confianza.

LONDON, UNITED KINGDOM

TOTAL BUILDING AREA: 2992 sq ft – 278 m²
EXTENSION AREA: 592 sq ft – 55 m² (main house) + 215 sq ft – 20 m² (garden room) //
27% of total area

The project was comprised of two parts: the extension of an existing townhouse and the creation of a garden pavilion with a south-facing patio. Orienting the house toward the garden and creating sightlines from deep into the old house, through the extension, and to the outdoors was an important priority. This was achieved by creating a large open space containing a living and dining area, and a kitchen at the rear of the house. The new arrangement was aimed at promoting interaction among the family members. The kitchen was designed as a box projecting into the garden with countertops that can be accessed from inside and out.

Ce projet comprenait deux parties : l'extension de la maison de ville existante et la création d'un pavillon de jardin doté d'un patio exposé au sud. L'orientation de la maison sur le jardin et la création de perspectives partant du cœur de la maison et allant, à travers l'extension, jusqu'aux extérieurs étaient des priorités majeures. Cet effet a été atteint par la création d'un grand espace ouvert qui accueille séjour et coin repas, et d'une cuisine à l'arrière de la maison. Cette nouvelle configuration visait à favoriser l'interaction entre les membres de la famille. La cuisine a été conçue comme une « boîte » donnant sur le jardin, les plans de travail étant accessibles de l'intérieur comme de l'extérieur.

Das Projekt bestand aus zwei Teilen: die Erweiterung eines bestehenden Townhouses und das Errichten eines Gartenpavillons mit einer nach Süden ausgerichteten Terrasse. Eine wichtige Priorität war die Öffnung des Hauses zum Garten und das Schaffen von Sichtachsen aus dem tiefen Inneren des alten Hauses durch den Anbau nach draußen. Ermöglicht wurde dies durch einen großen offenen Raum mit einem Wohn- und Essbereich und einer Küche im hinteren Teil des Hauses. Die neue Anordnung soll die Interaktion unter den Familienmitgliedern fördern. Die Küche hat ein kastenförmiges Design und wird in den Garten projiziert: Sie verfügt über Arbeitsplatten, die von innen und außen genutzt werden können.

El proyecto se compone de dos partes: la ampliación de una casa urbana existente y la creación de un pabellón de jardín con un patio orientado al sur. Las principales prioridades eran orientar la casa hacia el jardín y que, gracias a la ampliación, desde la zona más interior de la casa se pudiese ver el exterior. Se consiguió mediante la creación de un gran espacio abierto que contiene una sala de estar, comedor y una cocina en la parte trasera de la casa. La nueva disposición tenía la intención de promover la interacción entre los miembros de la familia. La cocina fue diseñada como una caja que se proyecta en el jardín con encimeras a las que se puede acceder desde dentro y fuera.

Photos © Marcus Peel

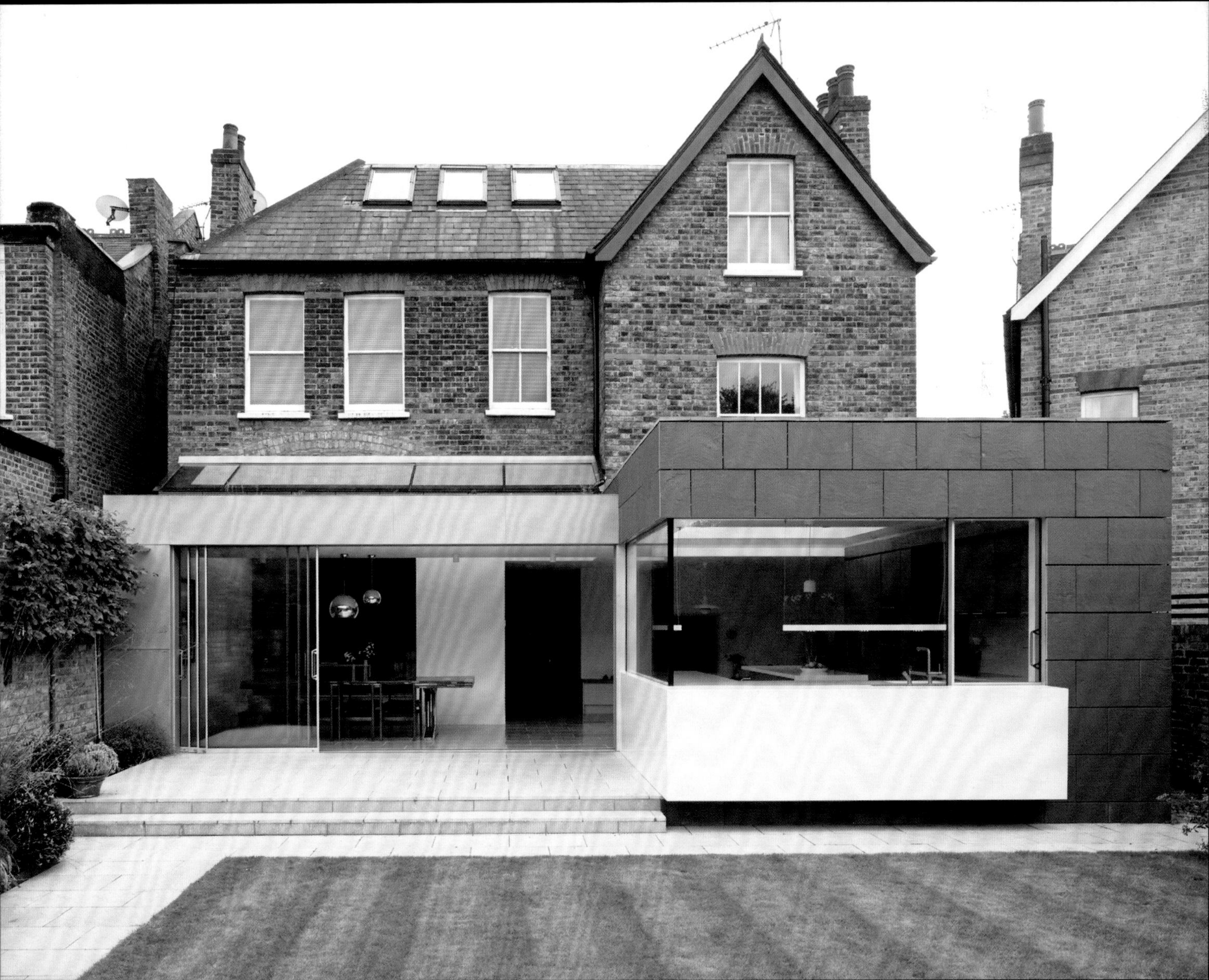

The original Victorian townhouse had well proportioned, light and spacious living spaces at the front, but a small and dark kitchen at the back, like many of the houses built in that era.

Le bâtiment d'origine, d'époque victorienne, était doté d'espaces d'habitation bien proportionnés, lumineux et spacieux à l'avant, mais avec une petite cuisine sombre à l'arrière, comme dans beaucoup de maisons construites à cette époque.

Das ursprüngliche viktorianische Townhouse hatte gut aufgeteilte, helle und geräumige Wohnbereiche im vorderen Teil, aber eine kleine dunkle Küche im hinteren Teil des Hauses, wie viele der Häuser, die in dieser Epoche gebaut wurden.

La casa original de estilo victoriano estaba bien dimensionada, con amplios y luminosos espacios en la parte delantera, pero con una pequeña y oscura cocina en la parte trasera, al igual que muchas de las casas construidas en la época.

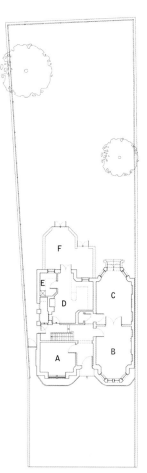

Original ground floor plan   0 1   5 m   New ground floor plan

A. Study   D. Kitchen
B. Pool room   E. Utility room
C. Living room   F. Conservatory

A. Study   E. Bathroom
B. Pool room   F. Dining room
C. Living room   G. Kitchen
D. Utility room   H. Garden room

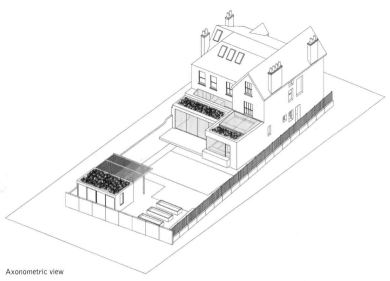

Axonometric view

The garden pavilion is used as an art studio. It acts as counterpoint to the house extension, creating a well-balanced composition.

Der Gartenpavillon wird als Kunstatelier genutzt. Er dient als Kontrapunkt zum Anbau und sorgt für eine ausgewogene Komposition.

Le pavillon de jardin fait office d'atelier d'artiste. Il sert de contrepoint à l'extension de la maison, ce qui crée une composition bien équilibrée.

El pabellón del jardín se utiliza como un estudio de arte. Actúa como contrapunto a la extensión de la casa, creando una composición bien equilibrada.

The architect's task was to transform once dark living spaces into the heart of the house, set around cooking and eating.

Der Architekt hatte die Aufgabe, einst dunkle Wohnbereiche mit den Schwerpunkten Kochen und Essen im Herzen des Hauses umzugestalten.

La tâche de l'architecte était de faire en sorte que les espaces autrefois sombres deviennent le cœur de la maison, organisés autour de la cuisine et des repas.

La tarea del arquitecto era transformar los espacios oscurosen el corazón de la casa configurados entorno a la cocina y al comedor.

MALBROOK HOUSE

A pavilion extension

LONDON, UNITED KINGDOM

TOTAL BUILDING AREA: 1485 sq ft – 138 m²
EXTENSION AREA: 301 sq ft – 28 m² // 20% of total area

The architectural concept for the project was to design a "pavilion" that neatly linked the existing house with the garden at the back of the property, whilst responding to the clients' wish to create a flexible family space that would connect them directly to the exterior. This new extension, whilst contemporary in form and use, uses traditional brickwork to link to the history of the existing building and area. Cor-ten steel vertical fins frame the paved exterior patio along one side. This material balances well with the old stock brickwork and yet, at the same time, feels sharp and contrasting.

Le concept architectural derrière ce projet était de concevoir un « pavillon » qui ferait un lien élégant entre la maison existante et le jardin à l'arrière de la propriété, tout en répondant au désir des clients de créer un espace familial modulable qui les relierait directement à l'extérieur. Cette nouvelle extension, quoique contemporaine dans sa forme et son usage, utilise la maçonnerie traditionnelle en brique pour faire le lien avec l'histoire du bâtiment et le quartier existant. Des ailettes verticales en acier Corten bordent un côté du patio extérieur pavé. Ce matériau est en bon équilibre avec les anciens parements et cependant, en même temps, crée un effet de netteté et de contraste.

Das Architekturkonzept für dieses Projekt bestand darin, einen „Pavillon" zu entwerfen, der eine harmonische Verbindung zwischen dem bestehenden Haus und dem Garten an der Rückseite des Gebäudes kreiert. Gleichzeitig sollte der Wunsch des Kunden nach einem flexiblen Familienbereich erfüllt werden, der die Familie direkt mit dem Außenbereich verbindet. Der neue Anbau mit zeitgenössischer Form und Verwendung nutzt traditionelles Mauerwerk, um auf die Geschichte des bestehenden Gebäudes und der Region Bezug zu nehmen. An einer Seite wird die gepflasterte Außenterrasse von vertikalen Lamellen aus Cortenstahl umrahmt. Dieses Material harmonisiert gut mit den alten Ziegelsteinen, ist aber gleichzeitig prägnant und kontrastierend.

El concepto arquitectónico del proyecto fue diseñar un "pabellón" que vinculase la casa existente con el jardín, en la parte de atrás de la propiedad, y que respondiese al deseo de los clientes de crear un espacio flexible para la familia que los conectase directamente con el exterior. Esta ampliación, aunque contemporánea en forma y uso, utiliza ladrillo tradicional como referencia a la historia del edificio original y de la zona. En el patio exterior pavimentado, destacan las lamas verticales de acero Corten que enmarcan el área en un lateral. Este material se equilibra a la vez que contrasta con los ladrillos antiguos.

TIGG+COLL ARCHITECTS

Photos © Andy Matthews

The existing late Victorian house had lost its character to various extensions. The approach for the new project was to replace these extensions with a new structure that would enhance rather than obscure the original style of the house.

La maison existante, datant de la fin de l'époque victorienne, avait perdu de son caractère au fil de diverses extensions. L'approche de ce nouveau projet consistait à remplacer ces extensions par une nouvelle structure qui mettrait en valeur le style original de la maison plutôt que de l'occulter.

Das bestehende spätviktorianische Haus hat seinen Charakter durch mehrere Anbauten verloren. Das neue Projekt hatte zum Ziel, diese Anbauten durch ein neues Gebäude zu ersetzen, das den ursprünglichen Stil des Hauses betont statt ihn zu verdecken.

La casa original de estilo victoriano había perdido su carácter en distintas ampliaciones. El enfoque de este nuevo proyecto era reemplazarlas con una nueva estructura que realzase en lugar de oscurecer, el estilo original de la vivienda.

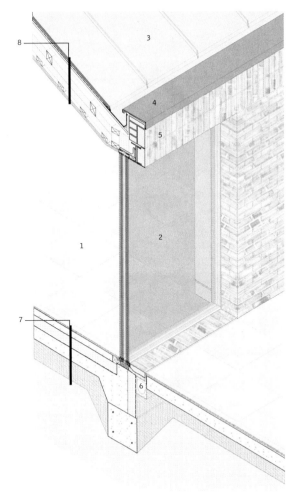

1. Royal Mosa 75 Tiles (262)
2. IQ Glass Solutions Sliding Door
3. Unweathered zinc roof
4. Unweathered zinc coping
5. Reclaimed stock bricks
6. Aco MultiDrain MD Brickslot
7. Floor build-up
   - 20 mm floor finish (large format 750 x 750 mm size by Royal Mosa
   - 5 mm Adhesive bed
   - 75 mm Heated screed
   - 500 gauge polythene VCL
   - 125 mm Celotex FF 4000 (or equivalent)
   - 1200 Gauge polythene DPM
   - 150 mm Ground bearing slab to structural engineer's detail
   - Min. 150 mm Compacted hardcore
8. Roof build-up
   - Unweathered zinc sheeting
   - Sheathing on 18 mm WBP plywood
   - 100 mm Ventilated cavity
   - 200 mm Composite steel/timber structure to structural engineer's detail
   - 100 mm Celotex FR5000 between rafters (or equivalent)
   - 100 mm Celotex FR5000 under rafters (or equivalent)
   - Taped joints to form VCL
   - 25 x 47 mm Softwood battens
   - 2 x 12.5 mm Plasterboard

Axonometric view. Technical section

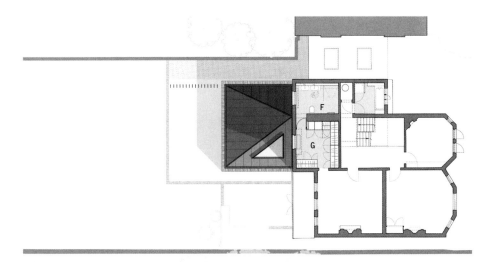

New first floor plan

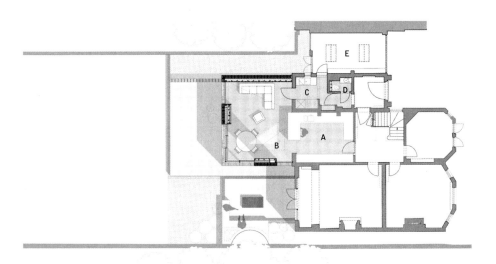

New ground floor plan

A. Kitchen   E. Garage
B. Kitchen extension F. En suite bathroom
C. Utility room   G. Dressing room
D. Powder room

Carefully placed glazed elements were positioned to take advantage of the sunlight as it moves across the building throughout the day, and to frame views out onto the garden.

Die sorgfältig platzierten Glaselemente wurden so angeordnet, dass sie das Licht der Sonne nutzen, die sich im Laufe des Tages um das Gebäude herum bewegt, und die Ausblicke auf den Garten umrahmen.

Des éléments vitrés placés avec soin ont été positionnés pour profiter de la lumière du soleil dans son parcours au travers du bâtiment durant la journée, et encadrer les vues sur le jardin.

Elementos acristalados situados en lugares estratégicos se aprovechan de la luz del sol conforme se mueve sobre el edificio a lo largo del día y enmarcan las vistas sobre el paisaje.

The linear light detail recessed into the ceiling accentuates the faceted internal soffit giving a soft glow that really lifts the space in the evening. The skylight brings light deep into the space.

Das lineare, in die Decke eingesetzte Lichtdetail betont die facettierte Deckenuntersicht im Innenbereich und verleiht ihr einen warmen Schimmer, der dem Raum am Abend eine besondere Atmosphäre verleiht. Durch das Oberlicht fällt Tageslicht bis tief in den Raum hinein.

Le détail des luminaires linéaires encastrés dans le plafond accentue le soffite intérieur à facettes en procurant une lumière douce qui relève véritablement l'espace. La fenêtre de toit y fait pénétrer la lumière en profondeur.

La línea de luz empotrada en el techo acentúa la zona interna de la estructura proporcionando un suave resplandor que ilumina el espacio al atardecer. Durante el día, la claraboya atrae la luz hasta el interior del espacio.

TRINITY HALL
Subterranean spatial solution

OXFORD, UNITED KINGDOM

TOTAL BUILDING AREA: 4230 sq ft – 393 m^2
EXTENSION AREA: 1130 sq ft – 105 m^2 // 27% of total area

This five-storey Victorian house originally belonged to Oxford University. Whilst its interior was subdivided into student flats, the building's original character remained intact. Still, much work needed to be done to adapt its interior to modern living. The existing building didn't have a proper cooking area, so a well-fitted kitchen was tailored to the lifestyle of the family, opened to the rear patio and to the garden beyond. In response to the need to bring more light into the house, a new skylight was placed above the main stairwell and another above the new family room and kitchen.

Cette maison victorienne de cinq étages appartenait à l'Université d'Oxford. Alors que son intérieur fut subdivisé en appartement d'étudiants, le caractère original du bâtiment demeura intact. Cependant, il fut nécessaire de faire beaucoup de travaux pour adapter son intérieur à un style de vie moderne. La maison existante n'ayant pas de véritable équipement culinaire, une cuisine a été spécialement conçue pour correspondre au style de vie de la famille, ouverte sur le patio arrière et sur le jardin juste derrière. En réponse au besoin de faire entrer davantage de lumière dans la maison, un nouveau puits de jour a été placé au-dessus de la cage d'escalier principale ainsi qu'un autre au-dessus de la nouvelle pièce à vivre-cuisine.

Das fünfstöckige viktorianische Haus gehörte ursprünglich zur Oxford University. Während wurde sein Inneres in Studentenwohnungen unterteilt, den ursprünglichen Charakter des Gebäudes blieb intakt. Dennoch brauchte viel Arbeit getan werden um das Innenre zu modernen Wohnraum anzupassen. Das bestehende Gebäude hatte keinen richtigen Kochbereich, sodass eine gut ausgestattete Küche auf die Bedürfnisse der Familie zugeschnitten wurde, die sich zur Terrasse hinter dem Haus und dem dahinter liegenden Garten öffnet. Um mehr Licht ins Haus zu bringen, wurde ein neues Oberlicht über dem Haupttreppenhaus und ein weiteres über dem neuen Familienzimmer und der Küche eingesetzt.

Esta casa victoriana de cinco plantas pertenecía originariamente a la Universidad de Oxford. Mientras que su interior fue subdividido en pisos de estudiantes, el carácter original del edificio se mantuvo intacto. Aún así, la adaptación del interior a los tiempos actuales exigió mucho trabajo. El edificio original no tenía una zona de cocina apropiada, por lo que se diseñó una cocina bien equipada adecuada al estilo de vida de la familia, que se abre al patio trasero y al jardín. La casa necesitaba más luz, por ello se diseñó una claraboya sobre la escalera principal y otra sobre la zona de estar y la cocina.

The building stands gracefully, boasting its original character. With high ceilings and nice proportions, the architectural essence remained intact, but the excessively compartmentalized interior needed an extensive refurbishment to make the place liveable as a single-family dwelling.

Le bâtiment a une allure gracieuse, dévoilant fièrement son caractère original. Avec ses plafonds hauts et ses belles proportions, son essence architecturale n'était pas affectée, mais l'intérieur compartimenté à l'excès nécessitait une rénovation importante pour adapter le lieu à la vie familiale.

Das anmutige Gebäude hat seinen ursprünglichen Charakter bewahrt. Mit den hohen Decken und den schönen Proportionen blieb die architektonische Essenz erhalten, aber der übermäßig unterteilte Innenbereich erforderte eine umfangreiche Sanierung, um den Platz als Einfamilienhaus nutzen zu können.

El edificio, que conserva todo su carácter original, rezuma elegancia. Su esencia arquitectónica se mantiene, gracias a los techos altos y proporciones armoniosas. Sin embargo, la división excesiva del interior obligaba a efectuar una gran reforma para convertir la casa en el hogar de una familia.

New second floor plan

New first floor plan

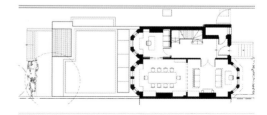

New ground floor plan

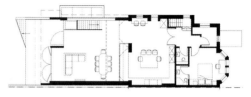

New upper basement floor plan

New lower basement floor plan

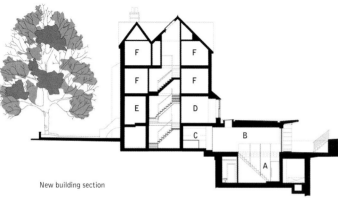

New building section

A. Games/cinema room   D. Study
B. Family room   E. Hall
C. Kitchen   F. Bedroom

The house now extends two floors below ground level: a bright and spacious kitchen and family room now occupy the original basement which was turned into the heart of the home; a new lower basement was designed to accommodate a games room and home cinema.

Das Haus erstreckt sich nun zwei Untergeschosse: Ein heller und geräumiger Küchen- und Familienraum belegt nun das ursprüngliche Untergeschoss, das zum Herz des Hauses umgestaltet wurde, und in der neuen darunter liegenden Untergeschossebene sind ein Spielzimmer und ein Heimkino untergebracht.

La maison s´étend maintenant deux étages en-dessous du niveau du sol : une cuisine et pièce de jour lumineuse et spacieuse occupent aujourd'hui l'ancien sous-sol qui est devenu le cœur de la maison ; un nouveau deuxième sous-sol a été conçu pour recevoir une salle de jeux et de cinéma.

La vivienda se extiende dos plantas bajo el nivel de calle: una luminosa y espaciosa cocina y una sala de estar ahora ocupan el antiguo sótano, que se ha convertido en el corazón del hogar; se diseñó un nuevo sótano más profundo para albergar una sala de juegos y de cine.

ELMS ROAD
Clapham Common Extension

LONDON, UNITED KINGDOM

TOTAL BUILDING AREA: 2895 sq ft – 269 m^2
EXTENSION AREA: 129 sq ft – 12 m^2 // 4.5% of total area

A basement remodel and extension of a semidetached Edwardian terraced house feature a minimalist design and a distinctive functionality, bringing together tradition and cutting-edge building technology. One of the main challenges was to create a structure or the extension that had the thinnest top edge possible to minimise the visual impact on the terraced house. The design successfully opens up the original plan formed by closed off and segregated rooms and creates a spacious open plan living area facing the garden. This living area has continuous flooring flush with an exterior patio that further enhances the open character of the design, which is an expression of contemporary lifestyles.

Un réaménagement du sous-sol et une extension d'une maison mitoyenne édouardienne présentent un design minimaliste et une fonctionnalité distinctive, associant tradition et technologie de construction de pointe. L'un des défis principaux était de créer une structure de l'extension dont la partie supérieure serait aussi fine que possible pour minimiser l'impact visuel sur la maison. Le design parvient à ouvrir le plan originel formé par des pièces fermées et cloisonnées pour créer une pièce à vivre ouverte et spacieuse donnant sur le jardin. Cette zone bénéficie d'un sol continu au même niveau que le patio extérieur faisant ressortir d'autant mieux le caractère ouvert du design, dans son expression de styles de vie contemporains.

Der Ausbau des Untergeschosses und die Erweiterung einer edwardianischen Reihenhaus-Doppelhaushälfte zeichnen sich durch ein minimalistisches Design und eine ausgeprägte Funktionalität aus und verbinden Tradition und hochmoderne Bautechnologie. Zu den größten Herausforderungen gehörte es, für den Anbau ein Gebäude mit einer möglichst dünnen Oberkante zu entwerfen, um eine visuelle Beeinträchtigung des Reihenhauses zu minimieren. Das Design öffnet das ursprüngliche Haus, das aus abgeschlossenen und isolierten Räumen bestand, erfolgreich und lässt einen großzügigen offenen Wohnbereich entstehen, der zum Garten hinausgeht. Dieser Wohnbereich hat einen kontinuierlichen, mit der Außenterrasse bündigen Bodenbelag, der den offenen Charakter des Designs unterstreicht, welches Ausdruck eines modernen Lebensstils ist.

La remodelación de la planta baja y la ampliación de esta vivienda pareada de estilo eduardiano destaca por su diseño minimalista y su funcionalidad, aunando tradición y tecnología arquitectónica de última generación. Uno de los principales retos fue crear una estructura de la extensión con los perfiles más finos posibles, para minimizar el impacto visual sobre la vivienda. El diseño abre con éxito el plano original formado por habitaciones cerradas y segregadas y crea una zona común abierta frente al jardín. Patio y zona de día comparten el mismo suelo, lo que refuerza aún más el carácter abierto del diseño: una expresión del modo de vida contemporáneo.

LBMVARCHITECTS

Photos © LBMVarchitects

The original layout of terraced houses is hardly suitable for a contemporary living style. They generally had small kitchens, which had a strictly functional purpose, separate rooms that formed a very tight and compartmentalized plan, and not much light.

La disposition d'origine des maisons mitoyennes ne se prête pas idéalement au mode de vie contemporain. Elles étaient généralement dotées de petites cuisines, qui étaient strictement fonctionnelles, de pièces séparées qui formaient un plan très resserré et compartimenté, et de peu de lumière.

Die ursprüngliche räumliche Aufteilung von Reihenhäusern ist für einen modernen Lebensstil kaum geeignet. Sie hatten üblicherweise kleine Küchen, die einen rein funktionalen Zweck erfüllten, und separate Zimmer, die für eine enge und stark unterteilte Raumanordnung sorgten, und waren nicht sehr hell.

Generalmente, el plano original de estas casas es difícilmente compatible con el estilo de vida actual. Las cocinas solían ser pequeñas y estar diseñadas exclusivamente para la preparación de alimentos; la existencia de habitaciones separadas formaba un plano compartimentado y estrecho y no tenía mucha luz.

Original front elevation

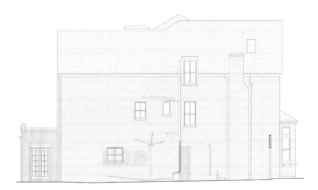

Original side elevation

Original rear elevation

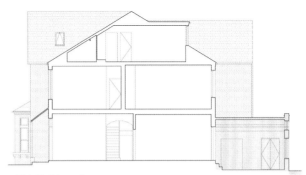

Original building section

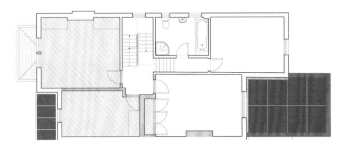

Original first floor plan

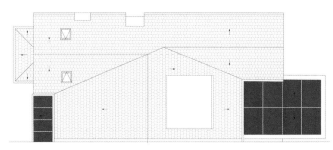

Original roof plan

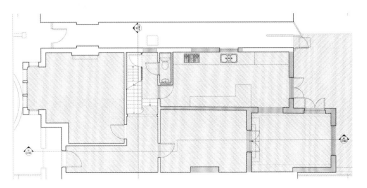

Original ground floor plan

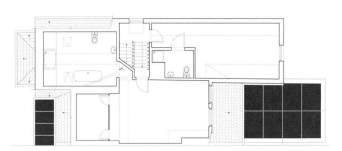

Original second floor plan

Original basement
floor plan

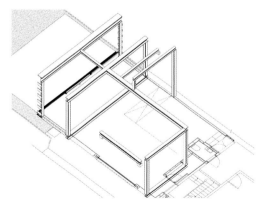

New structural scheme

New first floor plan

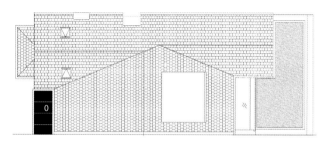

New roof plan

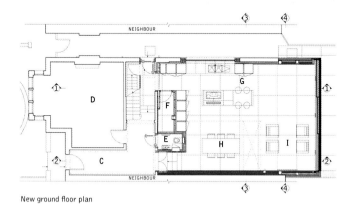

New ground floor plan

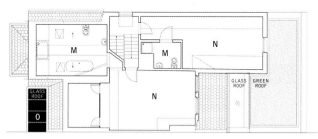

New second floor plan

A. Laundry room
B. Boiler room
C. Entry hall
D. Living room
E. Powder room
F. Walk-in-wardrobe

G. Kitchen
H. Dining area
I. Sitting area
J. Master bedroom
K. Master bedroom
L. Vestibule

M. Bathroom
N. Bedroom
O. Glass roof
P. Green roof
Q. Wardrobe

New basement floor
plan

0 1 2 m

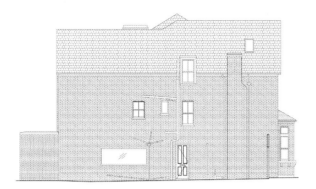

New side elevation

New rear elevation

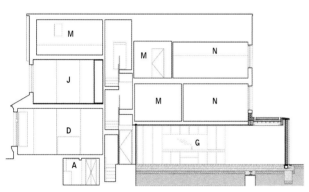

New section 1

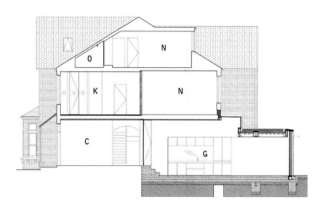

New section 2

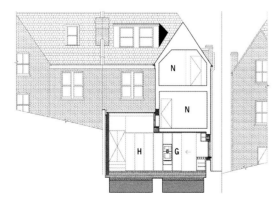

New section 3

New section 4

0 1 2 m

The kitchen design is in keeping with the minimalist space that contains it. The white surfaces reflect the light entering the space through the elevation facing the garden and through the large skylight.

Das Design der Küche berücksichtigt den minimalistischen Raum, in dem sie sich befindet. Die weißen Oberflächen spiegeln das Licht wider, das durch die zum Garten geöffnete Fassade und das große Oberlicht in den Raum heineinfällt.

La conception de la cuisine est en accord avec l'espace minimaliste dans lequel elle s'inscrit. Les surfaces blanches reflètent la lumière pénétrant l'espace par le biais de l'élévation qui fait face au jardin et à travers la grande fenêtre de toit.

El diseño de la cocina se coordina con el espacio minimalista que la contiene. Las superficies blancas reflejan la luz que penetra por el alzado frente al jardín y por el gran tragaluz.

LONDON, UNITED KINGDOM

TOTAL BUILDING AREA: 1819 sq ft – 169 m²
EXTENSION AREA: 366 sq ft – 34 m² // 20% of total area

The project consisted of the rearrangement of all the rooms of an existing townhouse to make the most of the available space, the design and construction of an extension along one side of the property toward the garden at ground level, and a loft conversion on the top floor. Because of the location of the house in a conservation area, a contemporary design approach was only feasible at ground level, whilst the loft conversion had to be in line with the local design guidelines.

Le projet consistait à remanier toutes les pièces d'une maison de ville existante pour mettre à profit l'espace disponible, concevoir et construire une extension sur un flanc de la propriété vers le jardin au niveau du rez-de-chaussée, et réaménager les combles au dernier étage. La maison étant située dans une zone de conservation du patrimoine, il n'était possible d'appliquer une approche contemporaine qu'au niveau du rez-de-chaussée, tandis que l'aménagement des combles devait être conforme aux normes de conception locales.

Das Projekt umfasste die Umgestaltung aller Zimmer eines bestehenden Townhouses, um den vorhandenen Raum optimal zu nutzen, den Entwurf und Bau eines sich zum Garten öffnenden Erdgeschossanbaus entlang einer Gebäudeseite und einen Dachgeschossausbau auf der obersten Etage. Aufgrund der Lage des Hauses in einem Denkmalschutzgebiet war ein zeitgenössisches Design nur im Erdgeschoss umsetzbar. Der Dachgeschossausbau musste den regionalen Gestaltungsrichtlinien entsprechen.

El proyecto consistió en la reorganización de las estancias de una casa adosada existente, para maximizar el espacio disponible. Además, incluía el diseño y la construcción de la extensión en la planta baja en un lateral de la propiedad con vistas al jardín y la reforma de la buhardilla en el piso superior. Esta última, debía hacerse siguiendo las directrices locales de diseño, al estar el edificio ubicado en una zona de conservación. En la planta baja, pudo seguirse un enfoque más contemporáneo.

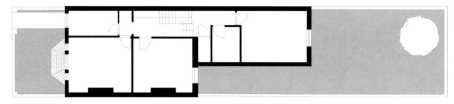

Original first floor plan

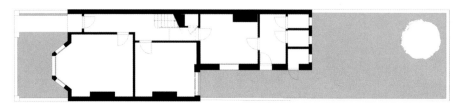

Original ground floor plan

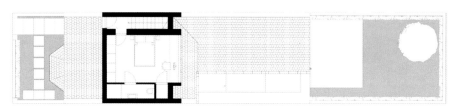

New second floor plan

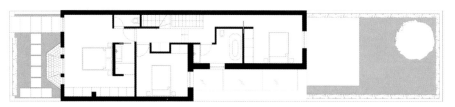

New first floor plan

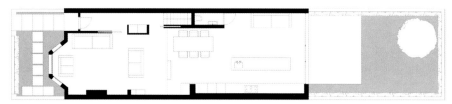

New ground floor plan

From the exterior, the ground floor extension is perceived as a distinct steel and glass structure that easies the transition between the existing brick building and the garden, whilst letting abundant natural light into the house.

Von außen wird der Erdgeschossanbau als ein individueller Stahl- und Glasbau wahrgenommen, der den Übergang zwischen dem bestehenden Backsteingebäude und dem Garten auflockert. Der Anbau lässt reichlich natürliches Licht in das Haus hinein.

Depuis l'extérieur, l'extension du rez-de-chaussée donne l'impression d'une structure distinctive d'acier et de verre qui favorise la transition entre le bâtiment de brique existant et le jardin, tout en apportant une profusion de lumière naturelle à l'intérieur de la maison.

Desde el exterior, la ampliación de la planta baja se percibe como una nítida estructura de acero y cristal que facilita la transición entre el edificio de ladrillo original y el jardín, a la vez que permite la entrada de abundante luz natural en la casa.

On the ground floor, substantial steel work allowed the design of an open plan kitchen and living area. The entire floor is set on two different levels because of the difficult ground conditions.

Im Erdgeschoss ermöglichte der Stahlbau das Design eines offenen Raums mit Küche und Wohnbereich. Die gesamte Etage liegt aufgrund der schwierigen Bodenbedingungen auf zwei verschiedenen Ebenen.

Au rez-de-chaussée, un ouvrage considérable en acier a permis la conception d'une cuisine ouverte avec coin repas. L'étage entier est fait de deux niveaux différents de par la configuration du sol.

En la planta baja, una importante obra de acero permitió el diseño de una cocina abierta y salón. La planta completa se asienta en dos niveles por las difíciles condiciones del suelo.

The new interior was stripped of all unnecessary ornament to focus on its essential spatial qualities. The spaces were enhanced by a minimal selection of materials and colour and by the effect of light on the different surfaces.

Der neue Innenraum kommt ohne unnötige Zierelemente aus, um den Fokus auf die wesentlichen räumlichen Funktionen der Räume zu legen. Er zeichnet sich durch eine minimale Material- und Farbauswahl und die Wirkung von Licht auf die unterschiedlichen Oberflächen aus.

Le nouvel intérieur a été débarrassé de tout ornement superflu pour se concentrer sur l'amplitude essentielle des espaces, relevée par une sélection minimaliste de matériaux et de couleurs et par l'effet de la lumière sur les différentes surfaces.

Se eliminaron todos los ornamentos innecesarios del nuevo espacio interior para centrarse en las cualidades espaciales esenciales de éste. Se pusieron en valor los espacios con una selección mínima de materiales y colores y con el efecto de la luz sobre las distintas superficies.

CUT AND FRAME

Home Extension and Writing Studio

LONDON, UNITED KINGDOM

TOTAL BUILDING AREA: 1916 sq ft – 178 m^2
EXTENSION AREA: 323 sq ft – 30 m^2 // 17% of total area

This extension must be understood as a visual connection between an existing two-storey semi-detached house and a former garden shed at the rear of the garden transformed into a writing hut. The design was driven by the requirements from the clients, a couple working from home, but with different occupations, one client being a children's book author, the other, a therapist. They both wanted separate spaces but somewhat connected. The tie between the house and the garden writing hut was therefore a key element of the project.

Cette extension doit être comprise comme une connexion visuelle entre une maison mitoyenne de deux étages et une ancienne cabane au fond du jardin transformée en cabanon d'écrivain. Le concept a été déterminé par les demandes des clients, un couple qui travaille à domicile, mais de professions différentes, l'un étant auteur de livres pour enfants et l'autre, thérapeute. Tous deux désiraient des espaces séparés mais avec une connexion. Le lien entre la maison et le cabanon d'écrivain constituait donc un élément clé du projet.

Der Anbau muss als visuelle Verbindung zwischen einer bestehenden zweistöckigen Doppelhaushälfte und einem ehemaligen Gartenhaus im hinteren Teil des Gartens verstanden werden, das zu einer Schreibhütte umgestaltet wurde. Das Design reflektiert die Anforderungen der Kunden, ein zu Hause arbeitendes Paar mit unterschiedlichen Berufen, ein Kunde ist Kinderbuchautor, der andere Therapeut. Sie wünschten sich separate Räume, die aber dennoch auf eine Weise miteinander verbunden sind. Die Verbindung zwischen dem Haus und der Schreibhütte im Garten war aus diesem Grund ein wesentliches Bestandteil des Projekts.

Esta ampliación debe comprenderse como una conexión visual entre una casa pareada de dos plantas y un antiguo cobertizo de jardín en la parte de atrás del mismo, transformado en un refugio para la escritura. El diseño se realizó teniendo en cuenta los deseos de los clientes: una pareja que trabajaba desde casa pero con distintas profesiones: escritor de libros infantiles y terapeuta. Ambos querían espacios separados pero conectados de algún modo. Por ello, el nexo entre la casa y el refugio de escritura del jardín fue un elemento clave del proyecto.

ASHTON PORTER ARCHITECTS

Photos © Andy Stagg

The interior of the existing house was completely remodelled and a series of historical, compartmentalised additions and alterations were removed to provide improved, interconnected living spaces.

L'intérieur de la maison existante a été totalement remanié et de nombreux ajouts et altérations historiques et cloisonnées ont été retirés pour y apporter des espaces à vivre améliorés et reliés entre eux.

Das Innere des bestehenden Hauses wurde komplett umgestaltet und es wurden verschiedene historische, uneinheitliche Erweiterungen und Umbauten entfernt, um verbesserte, miteinander verbundene Wohnbereiche entstehen zu lassen.

El interior de la casa existente se remodeló completamente. Se eliminaron una serie de adiciones y alteraciones anteriores que dividían el espacio, para ofrecer unos espacios comunes mejorados e interconectados.

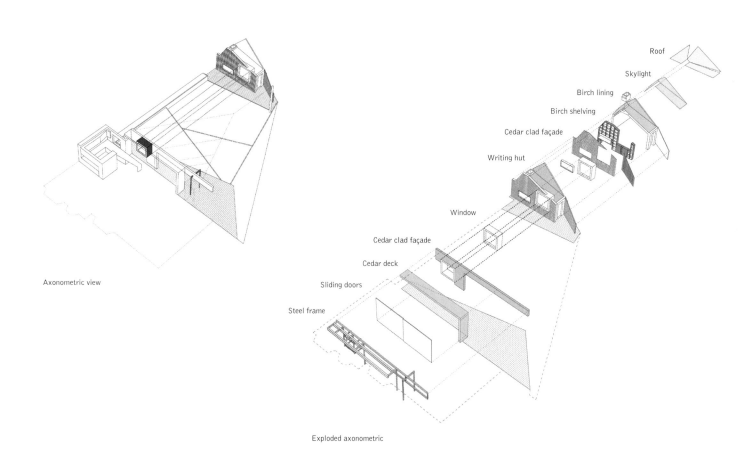

Axonometric view

Exploded axonometric

Roof
Skylight
Birch lining
Birch shelving
Cedar clad façade
Writing hut
Window
Cedar clad façade
Cedar deck
Sliding doors
Steel frame

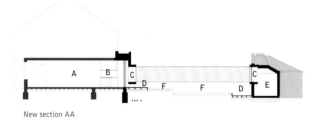

New section AA

A. Living room   D. Red cedar decking
B. Kitchen   E. Writing hut
C. Window seat   F. Lawn

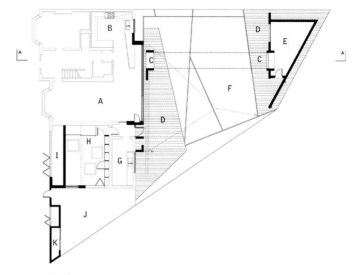

New floor plan

A. Living room   G. Utility room
B. Kitchen   H. Dining room
C. Window seat   I. Trash/recycling bins
D. Red cedar decking   storage
E. Writing hut   J. Outdoor living space
F. Lawn   K. Storage

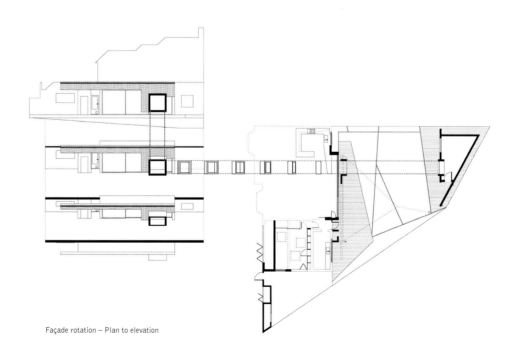

Façade rotation – Plan to elevation

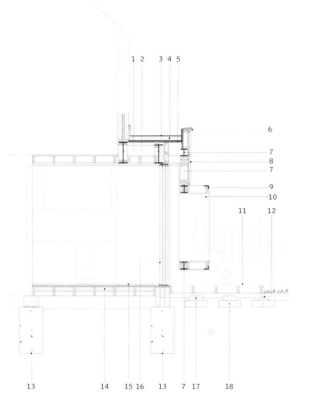

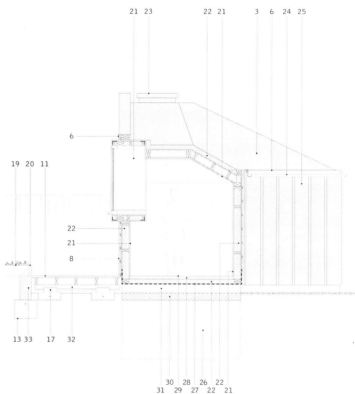

Building section details

1. 457 x 191 x 67 UB.
2. 406 x 178 x 67 UB.
3. Fiberglass roof in dark grey finish
4. 120 mm PIR Celotex XR4000
5. 18 mm WBP plywood
6. Fiberglass edge trim with lead grey finish
7. 152 mm uc frame
8. 100 x 20 cedar cladding with bevel cut to both edges
9. Angle frame to form seat
10. 3 mm aluminium sheet
11. 40 x 90 m western red cedar decking
12. 50 x 150 precast concrete edging set in concrete benching

13. New in situ mass concrete foundation
14. 100 mm PIR XR4000 insulation
15. Oak floor boards
16. Grey powder coated aluminium sliding doors
17. Precast concrete foundation pad
18. Gravel base
19. New horizontal terraced garden laid to lawn
20. 63 x 220 mm oak plan 2.6 m long) edging
21. 12 mm birch-faced lining
22. 100 mm styrene insulation
23. Grey powder coated aluminium skylight

24. 135 PVC half round gutter system (1:60 fall) in grey
25. Ebony stained 18 mm wbp cladding with external sw battens to vertical joints
26. In situ mass concrete lateral strips
27. Damp proof membrane
28. 65 mm sand cement screed
29. Rubber floor
30. Compressible board
31. In situ mass concrete slab with reinforcement mesh
32. Tanalised softwood joists
33. Masonry retaining wall

Framing elements reinforce the connection between hut and home. The main house has a floating seat of aluminium that becomes part of the internal seating of the house when the large glazed panels are slid away, and a garden seat at all times.

Rahmende Elemente verstärken die Verbindung zwischen der Hütte und dem Haus. Das Haupthaus verfügt über eine schwebende Sitzgelegenheit aus Aluminium. Sie wird zu einem Teil der Sitzgelegenheiten im Innenraum, wenn die großen Glaspaneelen zur Seite geschoben werden, und stellt jederzeit eine Sitzmöglichkeit im Garten dar.

Des éléments d'encadrement renforcent le lien entre le cabanon et la maison. Le bâtiment principal comporte un siège flottant en aluminium qui s'intègre à celui de l'intérieur de la maison lorsque les grandes baies vitrées sont ouvertes et sert de banc de jardin permanent.

Los perfiles refuerzan la conexión entre el refugio y la casa. La vivienda principal tiene un banco flotante de aluminio que forma parte del mobiliario interior cuando se abren los grandes paneles acristalados, mientras que puede usarse como banco de jardín en todo momento.

55

JACK'S HOUSE

An extension in dialogue with a victorian terrace and an industrial warehouse

MELBOURNE, AUSTRALIA

TOTAL BUILDING AREA: 1937 sq ft – 180 m^2
EXTENSION AREA: 581 sq ft – 54 m^2 // 30% of total area

The new extension offers a dialogue between two buildings of different eras, disconnected in style and function: an existing Victorian residence facing the street and an industrial saw-tooth warehouse on the rear boundary. The extension negotiates between the two buildings, stretching and tapering toward the saw-tooth brick building. Internally, it opens up from a double-loaded Victorian corridor to a spacious glazed room, with a brick wall on the boundary as a feature backdrop.
The existing street frontage was maintained without alteration, in keeping with the local character of hidden extensions to the rear of existing houses.

La nouvelle extension ouvre un dialogue entre deux bâtiments de différentes époques, sans connexion temporelle ni fonctionnelle : une résidence victorienne existante sur la rue et un entrepôt industriel à sheds sur la limite postérieure du lot. L'extension est une négociation entre les deux bâtiments, s'étendant et se rétrécissant dans le sens de l'entrepôt en briques. À l'intérieur, elle s'ouvre à partir d'un couloir victorien vers une pièce vitrée spacieuse, avec un mur de briques sur la limite comme toile de fond emblématique.
La façade existante a été préservée sans altération, dans la continuité du caractère local des extensions cachées derrière les maisons existantes.

Der neue Anbau lässt einen Dialog zwischen zwei Gebäuden verschiedener Epochen entstehen, die sich in Stil und Funktion unterscheiden: ein bestehendes viktorianisches Wohnhaus, das zur Straße hinausgeht, und eine Industriehalle mit Sheddach an der hinteren Grundstücksgrenze. Der Anbau vermittelt zwischen den beiden Gebäuden, er streckt und verjüngt sich in Richtung des Backsteingebäudes mit Sheddach. Im Inneren öffnet sich das zweibündige viktorianische Gebäude zu einem geräumigen verglasten Raum. Eine Ziegelsteinmauer an der Grundstücksgrenze bietet einen besonderen Hintergrund.
Die bestehende Straßenfront wurde ohne Veränderungen beibehalten. Dies ist im Einklang mit den Gepflogenheiten in der Region, in der es viele verborgene Anbauten an der Rückseite bestehender Häuser gibt.

La nueva extensión ofrece un diálogo entre dos edificios de distintos tiempos, desconectados en estilo y función: una residencia victoriana original junto a la calle y un almacén industrial con tejado en diente de sierra en la parte trasera de la propiedad. La extensión sirve de nexo entre los dos edificios, estirándose y estrechándose conforme se acerca al edificio industrial de ladrillo. Internamente, se abre desde un pasillo victoriano con puertas a ambos lados a una espaciosa habitación acristalada y con una pared de ladrillo en la linde como telón de fondo distintivo.
La fachada a la calle se conservó sin alteraciones, manteniendo el carácter local de esconder las extensiones en la parte de atrás de las casas originales.

FMD ARCHITECTS

Original east elevation

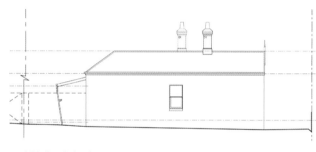

Original north elevation

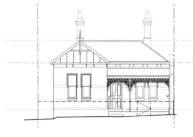

Original west elevation

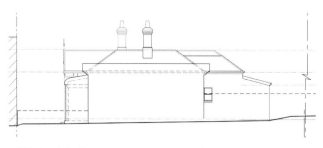

Original south elevation

------- · ------- Boundary line

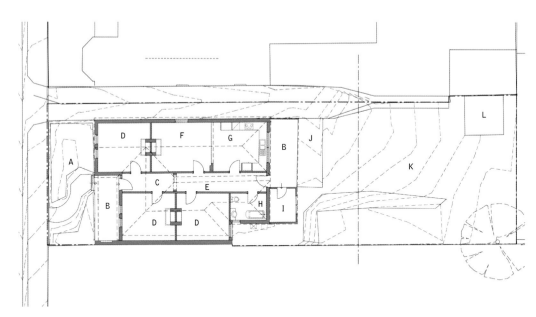

Original floor plan

A. Garden   G. Kitchen
B. Veranda   H. Bathroom
C. Entry   I. Laundry room
D. Bedroom   J. Paved area
E. Hall   K. Grass backyard
F. Lounge   L. Galvanized iron shed

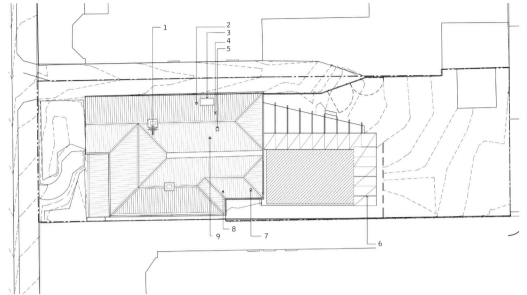

New roof plan

1. Existing antenna
2. Exhaust
3. New skylight as specified
4. Toilet vent
5. Range hood exhaust
6. Stiffeners to east canopy
   to engineer's specifications
7. Existing exhaust
8. Toilet vent
9. Dryer exhaust

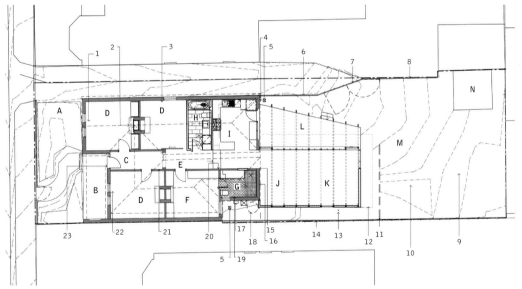

New floor plan

A. Garden
B. Veranda
C. Entry
D. Bedroom
E. Hall
F. Master bedroom
G. Master bathroom
H. Bathroom

I. Kitchen
J. Dining area
K. Lounge area
L. Terrace
M. Grass backyard
N. Existing
   galvanized shed

1. Boards retained for re-use
2. CT-06 to hearth
3. Patch and conceal existing A/C pipework
4. New tap
5. New storm water pit
6. New 2.5 m high paling fence (height to match existing)
7. Existing gate
8. Existing fence
9. Clothes line position to be confirmed
10. Site level to be confirmed
11. Retaining wall and AGI drain to be confirmed
12. Cantilevered canopy over
13. Relocated tap
14. Retaining wall to be confirmed
15. Patch plaster where nib removed
16. New sheet plaster over stud wall
17. New hot water system
18. New tank (by client)
19. New sheet plaster over stud wall
20. New skirting to match existing and follow line of step
21. Conceal thermostat conduit and patch as required
22. Patch flooring with retained boards
23. New weather strike to perimeter of existing door

New south elevation

9   8   7   6   5   4

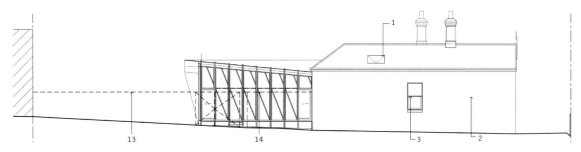

New north elevation

13   14   3   2   1

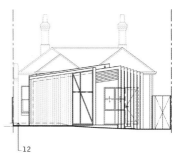

12

New east elevation

New west elevation

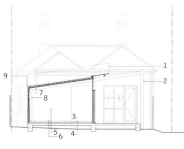

Cross section

—·—·—·— Boundary line

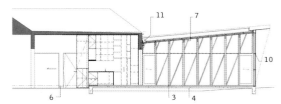

New partial longitudinal section

1. Canopy in front
2. Timber column to engineer's specifications
3. 70 mm topping slab for hydronic heating
4. Structural slab
5. Direct stick plaster to existing
6. Skirting as specified

7. Timber beam to engineer's details
8. Timber post (non-structural)
9. Rainwater head beyond
10. Steel angle lintel
11. Soaker gutter
12. Natural ground line shown dashed
13. Original fence
14. New fencing

Re-planning of the existing interior allowed the floor plan to improve its efficiency, thus ensuring the footprint of the new extension was minimized and the garden maximized.

Durch die Neuplanung des bestehenden Innenbereichs wurde die Raumaufteilung effizienter. So wurde die Grundfläche des Anbaus minimiert und die Gartenfläche maximiert.

Le réagencement de l'intérieur existant a permis au plan au sol d'améliorer son efficacité, limitant ainsi la superficie de la nouvelle extension et optimisant celle du jardin.

La replanificación del espacio interior permitió que el plano mejorase su eficiencia, asegurando que el espacio de la extensión se minimizara y el jardín se maximizara.

The interior detailing transitions from the Victorian craftsmanship to the modern plywood detailing as on moves through the spaces.

Beim Durchschreiten der Räume gehen Details der viktorianischen Handwerkskunst zu modernen Schichtholzdetails über.

Les détails intérieurs font la transition entre le savoir-faire victorien et les finitions modernes en contreplaqué à mesure qu'on avance dans les espaces.

Conforme nos movemos por las estancias observamos el cambio de los detalles artesanales victorianos a los remates modernos en contrachapado.

The extension allows the Victorian house to open itself up to natural light and ventilation and provide a large open plan living and dining area. The kitchen is also renovated and repositioned to improve its connection with the garden.

Durch den Anbau wird das viktorianische Haus deutlich heller und luftiger und bietet einen großen offenen Wohn- und Essbereich. Auch die Küche wurde renoviert und versetzt, um eine bessere Verbindung zum Garten herzustellen.

L'extension permet à cette maison victorienne de s'ouvrir à la lumière naturelle et à l'aération et procure un espace ouvert tenant lieu de pièce à vivre et coin repas. La cuisine est également rénovée et repositionnée pour améliorer sa connexion avec le jardin.

La extensión permite que la casa victoriana se abra a la luz natural y la ventilación a la vez que proporciona una gran área abierta para el comedor y zona de estar. La cocina también se renovó y reinstaló para mejorar su conexión con el jardín.

FENLON HOUSE
A new addition to an aging bungalow creates a unique balance

LOS ANGELES, CALIFORNIA, UNITED STATES

TOTAL BUILDING AREA: 960 sq ft – 89 m²
EXTENSION AREA: 76 sq ft – 7 m² // 8% of total area

A dilapidated 1920's bungalow has undergone a major remodel that brings new life to the old structure. The new addition to the front of the house forms a unique alliance with the remodelled existing house, whilst maintaining a stark differentiation. The frontispiece has been clad in a clear cedar, contrasting with the torched cedar that wraps the rest of the structure. The front addition integrates the house with the adjacent streetscape as it terraces down to the sidewalk and forms a long bench.

Un pavillon délabré des années 1920 a subi un remaniement majeur qui redonne vie à l'ancienne structure. La nouvelle structure contre la maison forme une alliance unique avec le bâtiment existant réagencé, tout en s'en démarquant de façon frappante. La façade est habillée d'un bardage de cèdre naturel qui contraste avec le cèdre brûlé couvrant le reste de la structure. Cet ajout intègre la propriété dans son contexte urbain, descendant en terrasse jusqu'au trottoir pour y former un long banc.

Ein baufälliger Bungalow aus den 1920er-Jahren wurde aufwändig umgebaut und hauchte dem alten Gebäude so neues Leben ein. Der Anbau an der Vorderseite des Hauses bildet mit dem umgebauten bestehenden Haus eine einzigartige Allianz, obwohl er sich gänzlich von diesem unterscheidet. Der neue vorspringende Gebäudeteil ist mit hellem Zedernholz verkleidet, während der Rest des Gebäudes mit verkohltem Zedernholz versehen ist. Der Anbau an der Vorderseite integriert das Haus in das angrenzende Straßenbild, denn er verläuft terrassenförmig hinunter zum Gehweg und bildet eine lange Sitzbank.

Una desvencijada casa unifamiliar de los años veinte ha experimentado una gran reforma que le ha dado nueva vida a la antigua estructura. La ampliación en el frente de la casa forma una alianza única con la vivienda existente remodelada, a la vez que mantiene una diferenciación rigurosa. El frontispicio se ha forrado de cedro natural, en contraste con el cedro carbonizado que envuelve el resto de la estructura. La ampliación en el frente integra a la vivienda con el paisaje urbano, al nivelarla con la acera mediante un gran banco.

The original gabled porch roof was removed leaving a large triangular opening in the roof, which has become a skylight, flooding the interior with natural light. The existing ceiling was removed to expose the original wooden roof structure.

La suppression de la toiture du porche à pignon d'origine a engendré une grande ouverture triangulaire qui a été transformée en puits de jour, inondant l'intérieur de lumière naturelle. Le plafond existant a été démonté pour dévoiler la charpente d'origine en bois.

Das ursprüngliche Giebeldach der Veranda wurde entfernt, wodurch eine große dreieckige Öffnung im Dach entstand. Hier wurde ein Oberlicht eingesetzt, das den Innenraum mit Licht durchflutet. Die bestehende Decke wurde entfernt, um die ursprüngliche Holzdachkonstruktion freizulegen.

La eliminación del tejado a dos aguas del porche dejó una gran apertura triangular en el tejado de la casa. Al convertirlo en lucernario se consiguió que la luz fluyera por todo el interior de la vivienda. También se quitó el falso techo para poder ver la estructura existente de madera del tejado.

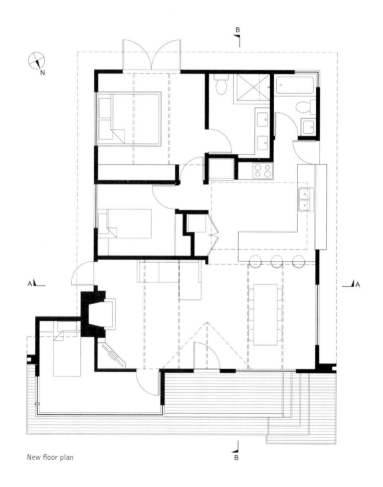

New floor plan

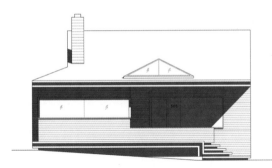

North elevation

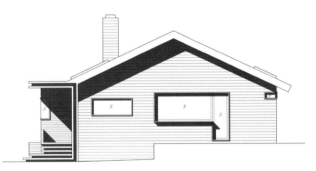

West elevation

New south elevation

New east elevation

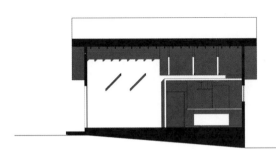

New section AA

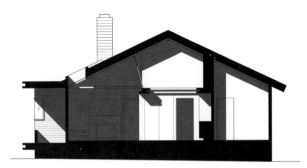

New section BB

The new walnut and teak finishes throughout are similar in tone with the existing wood, blurring the distinction between old and new. The simple combination of the wood and white plaster throughout is reminiscent of California mission architecture.

Die neuen Nussbaum- und Teakholzverkleidungen, die das gesamte Gebäude durchziehen, haben einen ähnlichen Ton wie das bestehende Holz, wodurch der Übergang zwischen Alt und Neu verwischt wird. Die schlichte Kombination aus Holz und weißem Putz erinnert an die Architektur der spanischen Missionen in Kalifornien.

Les nouvelles finitions en noyer et teck dans tout le bâtiment ont une tonalité comparable au bois d'origine, ce qui estompe la distinction entre l'ancien et le nouveau. La combinaison simple du bois et du plâtre blanc dans toute la maison rappelle l'architecture missionnaire de Californie.

Los nuevos acabados en madera de teca y nogal en toda la vivienda tienen un tono similar a la madera original, eliminando la distinción entre nuevo y antiguo. La combinación sencilla de madera y yeso blanco es una reminiscencia de la arquitectura californiana de las misiones.

Other areas of the interior are punctuated by a series of bespoke furniture that integrate everyday objects with the spaces they are in.

Weitere Innenbereiche werden durch eine Reihe von maßgeschneiderten Möbeln betont, die Alltagsgegenstände in die Räume integrieren, in denen sie sich befinden.

D'autres espaces intérieurs sont jalonnés d'une série de meubles sur-mesure qui intègrent les objets du quotidien dans les espaces qu'ils occupent.

En otras zonas del interior resaltan una serie de muebles hechos a medida que integran los objetos de uso diario con los espacios en los que se encuentran.

AUSTEN HOUSE POD
Flying Contemporary First Floor Extension

WINCHESTER, HAMPSHIRE, UNITED KINGDOM

TOTAL BUILDING AREA: 1765 sq ft – 164 m²
EXTENSION AREA: 215 sq ft – 20 m² // 12% of total area

Austen House was a recently converted dwelling on the site of the Old St. Swithun's School. Vacated in 1929, the school had outgrown the city centre location allowing the premises to be taken over by the library and then further development into residential dwellings. Austen House is part of this old development. The owners of the house wanted a clever and creative increase of space as well as abundant natural light and south facing orientation. An access way along one side of the property had to provide a right of passage for cars very occasionally, but it was possible to build out and create a new room over the top of this passage.

L'Austen House était une habitation récemment aménagée sur le site de l'ancienne école St. Swithun. Évacuée en 1929, l'école était devenue trop grande pour son emplacement du centre-ville. Les locaux ont alors été repris par la bibliothèque, puis transformés en habitations résidentielles. L'Austen House fait partie de cet ancien lotissement. Les propriétaires de la maison désiraient une augmentation de l'espace ingénieuse et créative ainsi qu'une profusion de lumière naturelle et une orientation vers le Sud. Une voie d'accès le long d'un côté du bâtiment devait permettre le passage très occasionnel de véhicules, mais il était possible de construire et de créer une nouvelle pièce au-dessus de ce passage.

Das Austen House war ein kürzlich zum Wohnhaus umfunktioniertes Gebäude auf dem Grundstück der Old St. Swithun's School, die 1929 geschlossen wurde. Die Schule war dem Stadtzentrum entwachsen und wurde so zunächst als Bibliothek genutzt und schließlich weiter zu Wohnhäusern umgebaut. Das Austen House ist Teil dieser alten Entwicklung. Die Besitzer des Hauses wünschten sich eine intelligente und kreative Vergrößerung des Raums sowie reichlich Tageslicht und eine Südausrichtung. Ein Zugangsweg, der entlang einer Seite des Gebäudes verlief, musste Autos sehr selten ein Durchfahrtsrecht gewähren, aber es war möglich, auszubauen und einen neuen Raum über diesem Weg zu errichten.

Austen House es una vivienda recientemente rehabilitada en el espacio de la escuela Old St. Swithun. La escuela creció hasta superar la capacidad de su ubicación en el centro de la ciudad y se desalojó en 1929. Sus instalaciones las ocuparon en primer lugar, la biblioteca y después se transformaron en viviendas residenciales. Austen House es parte de esta transformación. Los propietarios buscaban una ampliación creativa e inteligente que incorporase mucha luz natural y orientación sur. Una vía de acceso en uno de los lados de la propiedad debía quedar libre para permitir el paso de coches muy ocasionalmente, pero se podía construir por encima y crear una nueva habitación sobre ese pasaje.

ADAM **KNIBB** ARCHITECTS

Being within the town centre conservation area, the addition to the house had to stand out from the main building with materiality as well as design.

Da sich die Erweiterung im unter Denkmalschutz stehenden Stadtzentrum befindet, musste sie sich in Bezug auf Materialität und Design vom Hauptgebäude abheben.

La maison étant située dans la zone de conservation du patrimoine du centre-ville, cette annexe devait se détacher du bâtiment principal dans ses matériaux comme dans son concept.

Al estar en la zona de conservación del centro de la ciudad, la ampliación debía diferenciarse del edificio principal por sus materiales y su diseño.

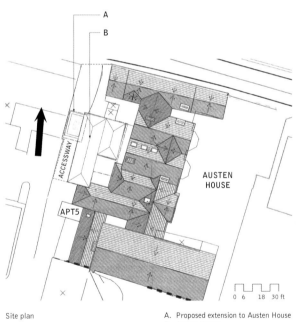

Site plan

A. Proposed extension to Austen House
B. Austen House

-- - — Site boundary
-- - — Ownership boundary
-- - - Granted rights of use over accessway

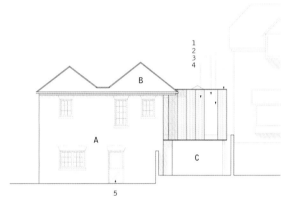

New north elevation

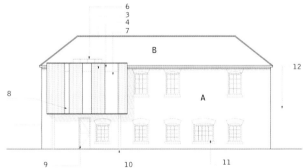

New west elevation

A. Original building
B. Original roof
C. Side accessway

1. PPC aluminium coping
2. Fixed window full height
3. Ceiling bulkhead (internally)
4. Vertical timber cladding units (600 mm bays)
5. Main entrance

6. Skylight (centre of roof)
7. Glazing fixed
8. First floor level
9. New glazed access door
10. Structural vertical slender columns
11. New window to kitchen/dining area to match adjacent windows
12. Boundary west wall to car park

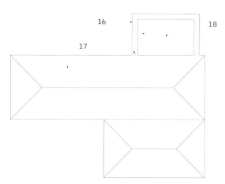

New roof plan

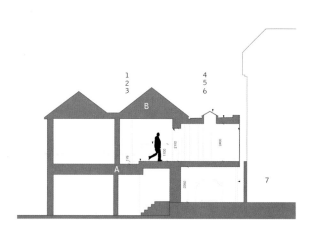

New north section

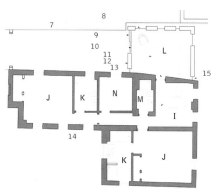

New second floor plan

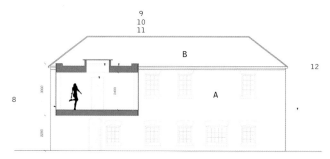

New west section

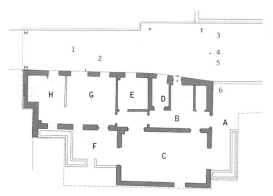

New ground floor plan

A. Main entrance	1. Side access	13. New access via full
B. Hall	2. New fixed window	glazed door
C. Lounge	3. Pod structural columns	14. New bridge walkway –
D. Powder room	4. Second floor extension	glass handrail
E. Study	outline above	15. Extension touches
F. Patio	5. New fully glazed door	existing building
G. Dining area	6. New opening for door	"lightly" with glass
H. Kitchen	7. Boundary wall	16. PPC aluminium coping
I. Landing	8. Glazed slot windows	17. Original tiled pitched
J. Bedroom	9. Juliet balcony	roof
K. En suite bathroom	10. Glass handrail	18. Skylight with small
L. Sitting area	11. Skylight/ventilation	opening sections for
M. Bathroom	above	ventilation
N. Bedroom	12. Solid wall – timber clad	

A. Original building
B. Original roof

1. New internal door
2. Glass balustrade
3. Walkway step up
4. Fixed window full height
5. Flat roof – drainage to existing

6. Skylight/ventilation
7. Slender steel post structure
8. Full height glazing and vertical timber cladding
9. New door way – glazing
10. Skylight
11. Flat roof
12. Boundary west wall to car park

The floating timber box which touches the building lightly (via glass slot windows) cantilevers out over the access way to give both a dramatic internal space, but also a prominent feature in the neighbourhood.

Der schwebende kastenförmige Holzbau, der das Gebäude (mittels Schlitzfenstern aus Glas) leicht berührt, befindet sich freitragend über dem Zugangsweg. Dadurch entsteht ein eindrucksvoller Innenraum, aber auch einer prägnanter Bau in der Wohngegend.

Effleurant le bâtiment (par le biais de fentes vitrées), le module en bois est en porte-à-faux au-dessus de la voie d'accès de façon à produire un espace intérieur étonnant, en faisant également un élément remarquable dans le quartier.

Unido al edificio central por unas ventanas alargadas, la caja de madera parece flotar sobre el pasaje de entrada para crear un espacio interuior sorprendente, pero sobre todo un marcado distintivo al vecindario.

Vertical timber cladding and large sections of glass have been designed to give a greater feeling of verticality and sense of place. With the tight nature of the site, the project was partially completed off-site to ensure minimal disruption.

Die vertikale Holzverkleidung und die großen Glasbereiche betonen die vertikale Ausrichtung und sorgen für eine bessere Anpassung an die Umgebung. Da das Grundstück beengt ist, wurde das Projekt teilweise an anderer Stelle fertiggestellt, um nur minimal zu stören.

Un bardage de bois vertical et de grandes surfaces vitrées ont été conçus pour amplifier l'impression de verticalité et le sentiment d'appartenance. Étant donné la nature compacte du lieu, ce projet a été en partie achevé hors-site pour minimiser le dérangement.

El recubrimiento en madera con listones verticales y las ventanas alargadas se han diseñado para dar una mayor sensación de verticalidad y de espacio. Debido al limitado espacio del solar, el proyecto se completó parcialmente en fábrica para minimizar molestias en el entorno.

FARMHOUSE ACHT5
Extension shows ambiguous synergy

BETUWE, THE NETHERLANDS

TOTAL BUILDING AREA: 3014 sq ft – 280 m^2
EXTENSION AREA: 1076 sq ft – 100 m^2 // 36% of total area

A small decaying farmhouse with a beautiful apple orchard was renovated extensively and added on to. The design strategy is aimed at maximizing the connection with the landscape, physically and metaphorically. As a result, a new single-storey annex stands alongside the farmhouse. The two buildings complement each other: the existing is massive, with few small openings and a hip roof; the addition stands low and light, with a flat roof and partially transparent. They form a striking pair visually bracketing decades of rural architecture and creating a compellingly simple dwelling for a lifestyle in the countryside.

Cette petite ferme délabrée avec son beau verger de pommiers a fait l'objet de rénovations considérables et de l'ajout d'une annexe. La stratégie du design vise à optimiser la connexion avec le paysage, physiquement et métaphoriquement. Il en résulte une annexe de plein pied qui se tient auprès de la ferme. Les deux bâtiments se complètent : celui d'origine est massif, avec peu d'ouvertures et une toiture à pans coupés ; l'annexe est basse et légère, surmontée d'un toit plat partiellement transparent. Elles forment un duo remarquable, évocation de décennies d'architecture rurale, créant une habitation d'une séduisante simplicité pour une vie à la campagne.

Ein kleines verfallendes Bauernhaus mit einem wunderschönen Apfelgarten wurde umfangreich renoviert und erweitert. Die Designstrategie sollte die Verbindung mit der Landschaft auf physische und metaphorische Weise maximieren. Das Ergebnis ist ein neuer einstöckiger Anbau neben dem Bauernhaus. Die beiden Gebäude ergänzen sich: Das bestehende Haus ist massiv und hat wenige kleine Öffnungen und ein Walmdach. Der Anbau hingegen ist niedrig und hell, er hat ein Flachdach und ist teilweise transparent. Zusammen bilden sie ein markantes Paar, das Jahrzehnte ländlicher Architektur umfasst und eine ansprechend schlichte Wohnstätte für ein Leben auf dem Land darstellt.

Este proyecto consistió en la renovación y ampliación de una pequeña granja en ruinas junto a un bello manzano. La estrategia del diseño es maximizar la conexión con el paisaje, física y metafóricamente. Como resultado, un anexo de una planta se ubica junto a la granja. Los dos edificios se complementan: el original es muy sólido, con pequeñas aberturas y un tejado a cuatro aguas; el anexo es bajo y ligero, con techo liso y parcialmente transparente. Visualmente forman una pareja singular uniendo décadas de arquitectura rural y creando una vivienda sencilla y convincente para un estilo de vida en el campo.

RESET ARCHITECTURE

The addition clearly shows that it is possible to reuse a derelict structure, whilst maintaining its original character. Juxtaposed contemporary buildings don't necessarily compete with an existing structure; they can actually coexist harmoniously, and balance each other.

Cette annexe montre clairement qu'il est possible de réutiliser une structure vétuste tout en préservant son caractère d'origine. Les bâtiments contemporains juxtaposés ne sont pas nécessairement en concurrence avec une structure existante ; au contraire ils peuvent coexister harmonieusement et s'équilibrer mutuellement.

Der Anbau zeigt deutlich, dass es möglich ist, ein verfallendes Gebäude wiederzuverwenden und dabei seinen ursprünglichen Charakter zu bewahren. Nebeneinanderstehende Gebäude müssen nicht notwendigerweise in Konkurrenz zueinander stehen, sondern können harmonisch koexistieren und ein Ausgleich füreinander sein.

El anexo demuestra que es posible reutilizar una estructura en ruinas, a la vez que se mantiene su carácter original. La yuxtaposición de edificios contemporáneos no genera necesariamente una lucha con la estructura existente; de hecho pueden coexistir armoniosamente y equilibrarse mutuamente.

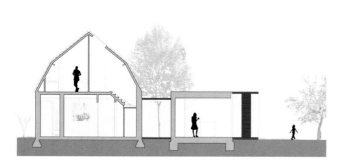

New building section

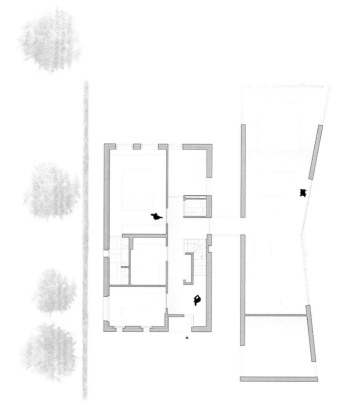

New floor plan

Two different housing archetypes are combined; a landscape-oriented, open-plan living space in the extension and a more enclosed layout, in the existing farmhouse. The architectural contrast between the farmhouse and its new added wing provides an ambiguous synergy.

Es werden zwei verschiedene Archetypen von Wohnraum kombiniert: ein der Landschaft zugewandter, offener Wohnbereich im Anbau und eine geschlossenere räumliche Aufteilung im bestehenden Bauernhaus. Der architektonische Kontrast zwischen dem Bauernhaus und dem neu hinzugefügten Gebäudetrakt lässt eine ambigue Synergie entstehen.

Deux archétypes de logement sont associés ; un espace ouvert, orienté vers le paysage à l'intérieur de l'extension et un agencement plus fermé dans la ferme d'origine. Le contraste architectural entre la ferme et sa nouvelle aile apporte une synergie ambiguë.

Aquí se combinan dos tipos distintos de vivienda. La ampliación destaca por ser un espacio abierto, orientado al paisaje y el edificio original, por su planta más cerrada. El contraste arquitectónico entre la granja y su ampliación proporciona una sinergia ambigua.

The historic background of the old farmhouse does not make the building a monument to be preserved at all costs. It is the commanding presence in its surroundings that makes the farmhouse distinctive and worth preserving.

Der historische Hintergrund des alten Bauernhauses macht aus dem Gebäude kein Denkmal, das um jeden Preis erhalten werden muss. Es ist die dominierende Präsenz in seiner Umgebung, die dieses Bauernhaus zu etwas Besonderem und Erhaltenswertem macht.

Le contexte historique de l'ancienne ferme ne justifie pas qu'elle soit préservée à tout prix. C'est sa présence imposante dans son environnement qui fait que cette ferme est originale et vaut la peine d'être sauvegardée.

Teniendo en cuenta sus antecedentes históricos, el edificio de la granja no es un monumento que deba conservarse a toda costa. Lo que lo hace único y digno de preservación, es su presencia dominante en el entorno.

The façades of the extension have an identical structure: there is a steel base and top edge separated by glass or timber infill. The black wooden slat infill is a reference to the traditional barn façades of the region.

Die Fassade des Anbaus hat eine identische Struktur: Das Fundament und die Oberkante aus Stahl sind durch Glas oder Holzausfachungen voneinander getrennt. Die Ausfachungen mit schwarzen Holzlatten erinnern an die traditionellen Scheunenfassaden der Region.

Les faces de l'extension ont une structure identique : une base et une arête supérieure en acier encadrant des éléments en verre ou en bois. Le remplissage en lattes de bois noires fait référence aux façades traditionnelles des granges de la région.

Las fachadas del anexo tienen una estructura idéntica: una base y perfiles de acero separados por cristal o paneles de madera. Las lamas de madera negra de los paneles son una referencia a las fachadas tradicionales de los graneros de la región.

URBAN BEAT
Renovation and extension of a townhouse

MONTREUIL-SOUS-BOIS, FRANCE

TOTAL BUILDING AREA: 1141 sq ft – 106 m²
EXTENSION AREA: 431 sq ft – 40 m² // 38% of total area

The main purpose of this project was to extend the area of the family home. The client had inherited the house from her grandfather. Rather than having the house tore down, she decided to work with what she had inherited. The process of adding a new floor to an existing structure is far more complex than starting from scratch. It is, however, a tool for urban densification, whilst maintaining a reference to the past. It was decided that the vertical extension was going to be a wooden structure for its lightweight quality, its fast assembly, and clean construction. It appeared to be the ideal response to the existing dense context. This method of construction allowed the owner of the house to remain in it during the duration of construction.

L'objectif principal de ce projet était d'agrandir la superficie de la maison familiale. La cliente avait hérité de la maison de son grand-père. Plutôt que de la faire démolir, elle a décidé de partir de ce qu'elle avait. Ajouter un niveau à une structure existante est un processus bien plus complexe que de créer un bâtiment de A à Z. Il s'agit, cependant, d'un outil de densification urbaine préservant parallèlement une référence au passé. Il a été décidé que l'extension verticale serait une structure en bois pour ses qualités de légèreté, son assemblage rapide, et sa construction propre. Elle est apparue comme la réponse idéale à la densité du contexte existant. Cette méthode de mise en œuvre a permis à la propriétaire d'y demeurer pendant la durée des travaux.

Der Hauptzweck dieses Projekts bestand darin, den Wohnbereich für die Familie zu erweitern. Die Kundin hatte das Haus von ihrem Großvater geerbt. Anstatt das Haus abzureißen, entschloss sie sich, mit dem zu arbeiten, was sie geerbt hatte. Eine neue Etage auf ein bestehendes Gebäude aufzusetzen ist viel komplexer als von Grund auf neu zu bauen. Allerdings ist diese Maßnahme gut für verdichtete urbane Wohngegenden geeignet und sie sorgt dafür, dass die Bezugnahme auf die Vergangenheit bewahrt wird. Für die vertikale Erweiterung wurde ein Holzbau gewählt, der mit seiner Leichtbauweise, der schnellen Montage und den klaren Linien überzeugte. Es war die ideale Antwort auf den bestehenden dicht bebauten Kontext. Die Baumethode bot dem Hausbesitzer die Möglichkeit, während der Baumaßnahmen im Haus wohnen zu bleiben.

El objetivo principal de este proyecto era ampliar el espacio de la vivienda familiar. Al recibir como herencia de su abuelo esta casa, el cliente decidió emprender su reforma en lugar de derruirla. Hay que tener en cuenta que el proceso de añadir una planta nueva a una estructura existente es mucho más complicado que empezar desde cero. Sin embargo, es una herramienta para la creciente densificación urbana que permite mantener al mismo tiempo las referencias al pasado. Se decidió que la extensión vertical sería una estructura de madera, por su ligereza, su facilidad de ensamblaje y su construcción limpia. Parecía la respuesta ideal a la densidad del contexto existente. Este método de construcción permitió que la dueña permaneciese en la vivienda

Rather than blending the extension with the existing white-rendered walls, the architects created two distinct volumes clad in different woods: poplar and pine. The result is a simple, yet expressive composition, which reflects the character of the area's architecture.

Plutôt que de fondre l'extension dans les murs enduits blancs existants, les architectes ont créé deux volumes distincts bardés de différentes essences : le peuplier et le pin. Le résultat est une composition simple, mais expressive, qui reflète l'architecture locale.

Anstatt die Erweiterung mit den bestehenden weiß verputzten Wänden verschmelzen zu lassen, haben die Architekten die Aufstockung in zwei verschiedene Teile unterteilt, die mit unterschiedlichen Holzarten verkleidet sind: Pappel und Kiefer. Das Ergebnis ist eine schlichte, aber ausdrucksstarke Komposition, die den Charakter der Architektur der Region widerspiegelt.

En lugar de unir la extensión con las paredes existentes recubiertas en blanco, los arquitectos crearon dos volúmenes distintos revestidos de dos maderas diferentes: chopo y pino. El resultado es una composición sencilla pero muy expresiva, que refleja el carácter de la arquitectura de la zona.

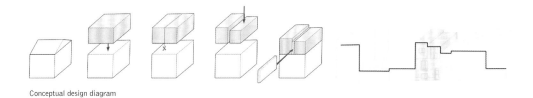

Conceptual design diagram

Original street elevation

New street elevation

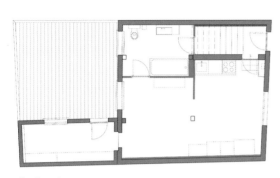

New floor plan

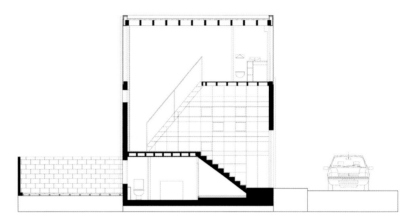

New building section

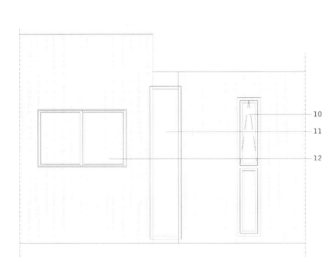

Partial wall elevation at extension

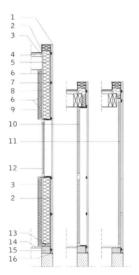

Section detail 1 Section detail 2 Section detail 3

1. Wall cap
2. Waterproof membrane
3. OSB shear wall panel
4. Metal decking
5. Top runner
6. Glass wool insulation
7. Furring strip
8. Wood siding
9. Facing material
10. Oscillating frame
11. Fixed frame
12. Sliding frame
13. Bottom runner
14. Flooring
15. Masonry base
16. Zinc flashing

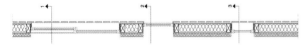

Partial plan detail at extension

97

The contemporary language of the exterior treatment of the addition permeates into the interior, where light and clean lines predominate.

Die moderne Sprache der äußeren Gestaltung des Anbaus durchdringt auch den Innenraum, in dem Licht und klare Linien vorherrschen.

Le langage contemporain du traitement extérieur de l'ajout s'infiltre jusque dans l'intérieur, où prédominent la lumière et les lignes épurées.

El lenguaje contemporáneo del exterior penetra en el interior, donde siguen predominando la luz y las líneas puras.

THE CAKE HOUSE
Colourful stratification

PISTOIA, ITALY

TOTAL BUILDING AREA: 5005 sq ft – 465 m²
EXTENSION AREA: 914 sq ft – 85 m² // 18,5% of total area

The existing house is located in a residential area mainly formed by single and two-story houses with gardens. The client needed to have the area of his house increased by twenty per cent, without reducing the garden area. After a preliminary analysis, it was decided to act on the southwest side of the house, which faces the garden and the town beyond. The idea was not to simply expand the existing structure, but rather to create an addition that would stand out from the original. At this point, the concept revealed itself as an arithmetic work of addition and subtraction.

Le bâtiment existant est situé dans une zone résidentielle formée majoritairement de maisons d'un à deux étages avec jardin. Le client voulait que la superficie de sa propriété soit doublée de vingt pour cent, sans réduire celle du jardin. Après une analyse préliminaire, il a été décidé d'agir sur la face Sud-Ouest de la maison, qui fait face au jardin et, plus loin, à la ville. L'idée n'était pas simplement d'agrandir la structure existante, mais plutôt de créer un ajout qui se démarquerait de l'originale. À ce stade, le design a consisté en un travail arithmétique d'additions et de soustractions.

Das bestehende Haus liegt in einer Wohngegend, die hauptsächlich aus zweistöckigen Häusern mit Gärten besteht. Der Kunde brauchte eine zwanzigprozentige Vergrößerung des Wohnbereichs, ohne den Gartenbereich zu verkleinern. Nach einer ersten Analyse wurde beschlossen, an der Südwestseite des Hauses zu agieren, die sich zum Garten und zur dahinter liegenden Stadt öffnet. Das Konzept bestand nicht darin, den bestehenden Bau einfach zu erweitern, sondern eine Erweiterung anzufertigen, die sich von dem ursprünglichen Haus abhebt. An dieser Stelle offenbarte sich das Konzept als arithmetische Arbeit des Addierens und Substrahierens.

La casa original está ubicada en una zona residencial formada por viviendas de una o dos plantas con jardín. El cliente necesitaba aumentar la superficie de la edificación un veinte por ciento sin reducir la superficie de jardín. Después de un análisis preliminar, se decidió intervenir en la zona sudoeste de la casa, con vistas al jardín y a la ciudad. La idea, más que ampliar la estructura existente, era crear un añadido que destacara del original. En este punto, el concepto se reveló como un trabajo aritmético de suma y resta.

PROGETTOSPORE

A section of the existing building was removed in order to create a more appropriate support for the addition and facilitate the integration of the addition with the complex massing of the house.

Ein Teil des bestehenden Gebäudes wurde entfernt, um ein geeigneteres Auflager für die Erweiterung zu erhalten und um die Integration der Aufstockung in den komplexen Baukörper des Hauses zu erleichtern.

Une portion du bâtiment existant a été retirée pour créer un support plus adapté à l'ajout et faciliter l'intégration de celui-ci dans le volume complexe de la maison.

Se eliminó una sección del edificio original para crear un soporte más adecuado para la ampliación y para facilitar laintegración de esta en la compleja volumetría de la casa.

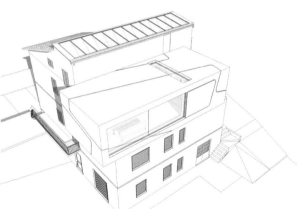

New building perspectives

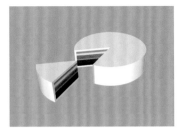

Step 1:
A cake

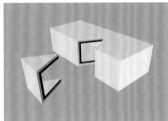

Step 2:
- The cake inspires the addition's volumetric design

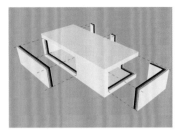

step 3:
- The slicing of the "cake" (windows and doors) reveals the layered filling

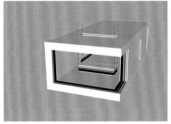

Step 4:
- A slice becomes the kitchen island

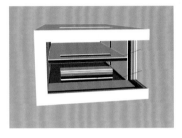
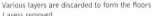

Step 5:
- Various layers are discarded to form the floors
- Layers removed
- Floor

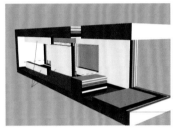

Step 6:
- Various layers are discarded to form wall units
- Layers removed

Step 7:
- Various layers are discarded to form sliding shutters

Step 8a:
- Identification of superfluous parts of the existing building

Step 8b:
- Removal of the superfluous parts

Step 8c:
- Insertion of the "cake"

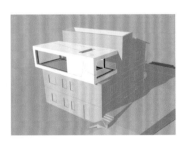

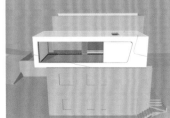

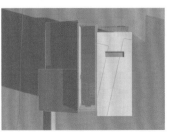

Different views of the house addition

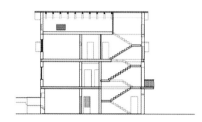

Original longitudinal section

Original cross section

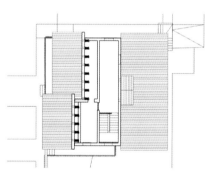

Original second floor plan

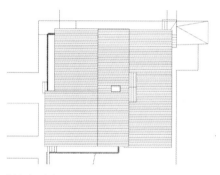

Original roof plan

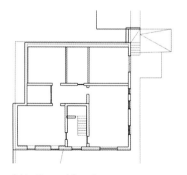

Original basement floor plan

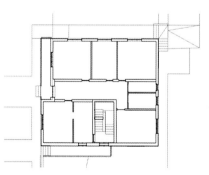

Original ground floor plan

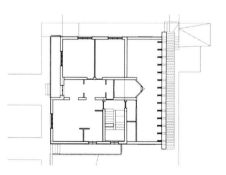

Original first floor plan

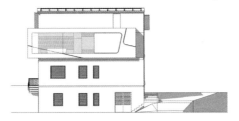

New west elevation

New east elevation

New north elevation

New south elevation

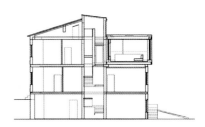

New cross section

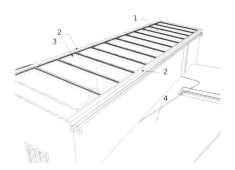

Views of addition's building components

1. Beams to support glazing
2. Insulated flashing
3. Glass pane
4. Reinforced glass
   (walkable)

Views of addition's steel frame

New first floor plan

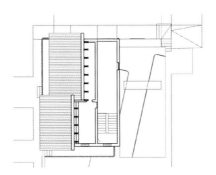

New second floor plan

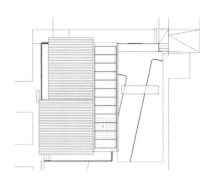

New roof plan

During the design process, the architects noticed that some layer cakes had the kind of structure they were looking for: a simple form at first, this structure, composed of various layers, can be altered by subtracting parts of different depths in order to create a more complex form.

Während des Entwurfsprozesses bemerkten die Architekten, dass einige Schichtkuchen die Art von Struktur hatten, nach der sie suchten: eine Struktur bestehend aus verschiedenen Schichten, die auf den ersten Blick schlicht erscheint, aber durch das Wegnehmen von Teilen unterschiedlicher Tiefe verändert und zu einer komplexeren Form werden kann.

Pendant la conception, les architectes ont remarqué que certaines pâtisseries avaient le type de structure qu'ils recherchaient : forme simple au premier regard, cette structure, composée de plusieurs couches, peut être altérée en en retirant des parties de différentes profondeurs pour créer une forme plus complexe.

Durante el proceso de diseño, los arquitectos se dieron cuenta de que algunas tartas con capas tenían el tipo de estructura que estaban buscando: una forma simple en primera instancia, compuesta de varias capas, que podía alterarse sustrayendo partes de distinta profundidad para crear una forma más compleja.

POWER HOUSE

A new floor from nowhere

LONDON, UNITED KINGDOM

TOTAL BUILDING AREA: 2422 sq ft – 225 m^2
EXTENSION AREA: 872 sq ft – 81 m^2 // 36% of total area

A typical Victorian terraced house takes a new direction with a highly sculptural timber clad rear extension. The scheme was inspired by the clients' love of the outdoors and a taste for Nordic design. A whole new lower ground floor level has been created beneath the original house. This has an open plan where a variety of activities—cooking, dining, and relaxing—can all take place simultaneously in a flexible arrangement for a growing family. Fully glazed folding doors give direct access to the garden deck.

Une maison mitoyenne typique de l'époque victorienne prend une nouvelle orientation grâce à une extension arrière tout-à-fait monumentale recouverte d'un bardage en bois. Ce projet a été inspiré par la passion des clients pour le plein air et leur goût pour le design scandinave. Un sous-sol entier a été nouvellement créé sous la maison d'origine. Il contient une pièce ouverte où toutes sortes d'activités – cuisine, dîners, et détente – peuvent avoir lieu simultanément dans une organisation modulable pour une famille qui s'agrandit. Des portes pliantes entièrement vitrées donnent directement accès à la terrasse extérieure.

Ein typisches viktorianisches Reihenhaus schlägt mit einem sehr skulpturalen holzverkleideten Anbau eine neue Richtung ein. Der Entwurf wurde von der Naturliebe des Kunden und einer Vorliebe für nordisches Design inspiriert. Neben dem ursprünglichen Haus wurde eine neue Erdgeschossebene errichtet, die offen gestaltet ist. Hier können in einer flexiblen Anordnung für wachsende Familien gleichzeitig verschiedene Aktivitäten – Kochen, Essen und Entspannen – stattfinden. Flügeltüren aus Glas bieten direkten Zugang zum Gartenbereich.

Una escultural extensión trasera con revestimiento de madera da un nuevo rumbo a una típica casa pareada de estilo victoriano. Al cliente le gustan los espacios exteriores y el diseño nórdico y estas dos características inspiraron el proyecto. Se creó una planta en semisótano por debajo de la casa original. Una zona abierta ideada para una familia en crecimiento que permite realizar toda una serie de actividades – cocinar, comer y relajarse– de forma simultánea. Las puertas correderas acristaladas dan acceso directo al patio y al jardín.

PAUL ARCHER DESIGN

This typical London Victorian terraced house offers a glimpse of the past, lending character, while at the same time adapting to current needs. The new design encompasses a new lower ground floor underneath the original house that has become a focal area for various activities such as cooking, dining and entertaining.

Cette maison mitoyenne londonienne typique de l'ère victorienne ouvre une fenêtre sur le passé, ce qui lui confère un certain caractère, tout en s'adaptant aux besoins actuels. Dans cette nouvelle conception, un deuxième sous-sol créé sous la maison d'origine est devenu une zone focale pour diverses activités telles que la cuisine, les dîners ou les réceptions.

Dieses typische Londoner Reihenhaus im Viktorianischen Stil bietet einen Blick in die Vergangenheit, was ihm Charakter verleiht, und ist zugleich an aktuelle Bedürfnisse angepasst. Der neue Entwurf schließt ein neues Untergeschoss unter dem ursprünglichen Haus ein, das nun für vielerlei Aktivitäten, wie Kochen, Essen und Unterhaltung, eine zentrale Rolle spielt.

Esta típica casa pareada londinense de estilo victoriano ofrece un destello del pasado, lleno de carácter, al mismo tiempo que se adapta a las necesidades actuales. Este nuevo diseño incluye una nueva planta en semisótano que es el punto central para distintas actividades como cocinar, comer o socializar.

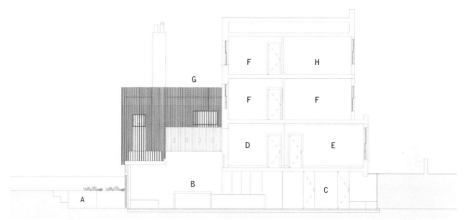

New building section

A. BBQ area
B. Breakfast bar
C. Play/TV area
D. Rear reception
E. Front reception
F. Bedroom
G. Terrace
H. Master bedroom

0 1 2 3 4 5m

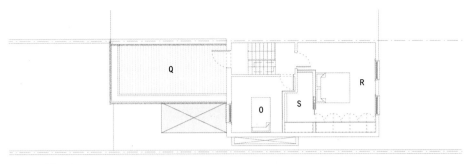

New second floor plan

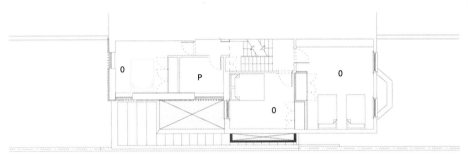

New first floor plan

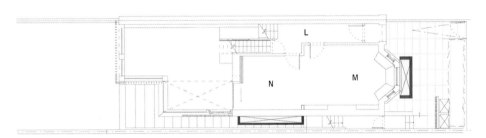

New ground floor plan

New lower ground floor plan

A. Patio
B. BBQ area
C. Living area
D. Dining area
E. Breakfast bar
F. Kitchen
G. Utility room
H. Pantry
I. Powder room
J. Play/TV area

K. Storage
L. Entry hall
M. Front reception
N. Rear reception
O. Bedroom
P. Bathroom
Q. Terrace
R. Master bedroom
S. En suite

0 1 2 3 4 5 m

The upper floors of the extension are clad with a skin of Douglas fir battens, which run both inside and out as exterior cladding and interior wall lining, emphasising the interplay between volumes.

Die Böden im Obergeschoss des Anbaus sind mit Douglasie-Dielen verkleidet, die sowohl im Innen- als auch im Außenbereich für Bodenverkleidungen und im Innenbereich außerdem für Wandverkleidungen eingesetzt wurden, was das Zusammenspiel zwischen den Räumen betont.

Les étages supérieurs de l'extension sont bardés de volige en Douglas dehors comme dedans sous forme de bardage extérieur et de doublage des murs intérieurs, ce qui met en valeur l'interaction entre les volumes.

Los pisos superiores de la extensión están revestidos de una piel de listones de pino de Oregón, que se extiende tanto en el interior, forrando las paredes, como en el exterior, revistiendo los muros, enfatizando la interrelación entre los volúmenes.

Wood is put to striking effect and is abundant in all aspects of the scheme from the signature linear cladding, external decking, interior floors, storage spaces disguised as walls and bench seating, and as a kitchen island with breakfast bar.

Holz kommt voll zur Geltung und findet sich in allen Aspekten des Entwurfs wieder: in der linearen Verkleidung, die das Gebäude auszeichnet, den Bodenbelägen im Außenbereich, den Böden im Innenbereich, den Stauräumen, die wie Wände und Sitzbänke aussehen, und der Kochinsel, die sich über die gesamte Länge der Küche erstreckt.

L'utilisation du bois est particulièrement remarquable et abonde dans tous ses aspects, du bardage linéaire distinctif à la terrasse extérieure, en passant par les sols intérieurs, les rangements invisibles déguisés en bancs, et comme îlot central avec tablette de petit déjeuner.

La madera produce un efecto llamativo y abunda en todos los aspectos del programa, desde el revestimiento lineal distintivo, pasando por el entarimado exterior, los suelos de la vivienda, espacios de almacenamiento ocultos en las paredes y el banco, hasta la isla de cocina con barra de desayuno.

The focal point of the new house is a spacious double-height kitchen and dining area at the rear of the property, which is created by the interplay of interlocking volumes made of frameless glass panels and linear timber panels.

Das Zentrum des neuen Hauses bilden die Küche und der Essbereich mit doppelter Raumhöhe im rückseitigen Teil des Gebäudes. Die Rückseite besteht aus einem Zusammenspiel von verschachtelten ungerahmten Glasscheiben und linearen Holzpaneelen.

Le point de mire de la nouvelle maison est une cuisine spacieuse en double hauteur avec un coin repas située à l'arrière de la propriété, qui est issue de l'interaction de volumes faits de panneaux vitrés à cadre masqué et de panneaux de bois linéaires imbriqués les uns dans les autres.

El punto central de la nueva casa es la zona espaciosa y de doble altura donde se encuentran la cocina y el comedor, en la parte de atrás de la vivienda, que se crea por la interacción de volúmenes conectados hechos de paneles de cristal sin marcos y paneles lineales de madera.

JIMI HOUSE

A home for art

LONDON, UNITED KINGDOM

TOTAL BUILDING AREA: 1938 sq ft – 180 m²
EXTENSION AREA: 43 sq ft – 4 m² // 2.5% of total area

The remodel and extension of a Victorian terraced house opens up its interior spaces to the garden, brings in daylight, and provides clear sight lines for the display of the owners' art collection. The added space neatly accommodates a modern light-filled galley kitchen with openings into a new spacious dining area and access to the garden. A clear layout and various design elements such as a full height glazed pivot door and glass balustrade on the upper ground level establish visual connections between the different spaces as well as between the interior and the exterior.

Le réagencement et l'extension d'une maison mitoyenne d'époque victorienne permet d'ouvrir ses espaces intérieurs sur le jardin, de faire entrer la lumière du jour, et d'offrir des perspectives dégagées pour exposer la collection d'œuvres d'art du propriétaire. Cet espace supplémentaire accueille élégamment une cuisine moderne et lumineuse avec des ouvertures vers un nouveau coin repas spacieux et un accès au jardin. Un agencement clair et divers éléments de design comme une porte pivotante entièrement vitrée et une balustrade en verre à l'étage supérieur établissent des connexions visuelles entre les différents espaces ainsi qu'entre l'intérieur et l'extérieur.

Der Um- und Ausbau des viktorianischen Reihenhauses öffnet seine Innenräume zum Garten, lässt Tageslicht hinein und bietet klare Sichtachsen zur Präsentation der Kunstsammlung des Kunden. Der zusätzliche Raum ist klar aufgeteilt und beherbergt einen lichtdurchfluteten Küchenbereich mit einer modernen Küchenzeile, die sich zum neuen geräumigen Essbereich öffnet und Zugang zum Garten bietet. Das klare Layout und verschiedene Designelemente, wie eine Drehtür aus Glas und Glasbalustraden im Obergeschoss schaffen lassen visuelle Verbindungen zwischen den unterschiedlichen Räumen sowie dem Innen- und Außenbereich entstehen.

La remodelación y ampliación de una casa adosada victoriana abre su espacio interior al jardín, atrae la luz natural y proporciona un amplio campo visual para la exposición de la colección de arte del dueño. El espacio añadido alberga una moderna cocina en paralelo llena de luz con aperturas a la nueva y espaciosa zona de comedor y acceso al jardín. Un plano limpio y varios elementos de diseño —como una puerta pivotante acristalada que llega del suelo al techo y una balaustrada de cristal en la zona alta de la planta baja— establecen conexión visual entre los distintos espacios así como entre el interior y el exterior.

PAUL ARCHER DESIGN

Photos © Alexander James and Paul Archer

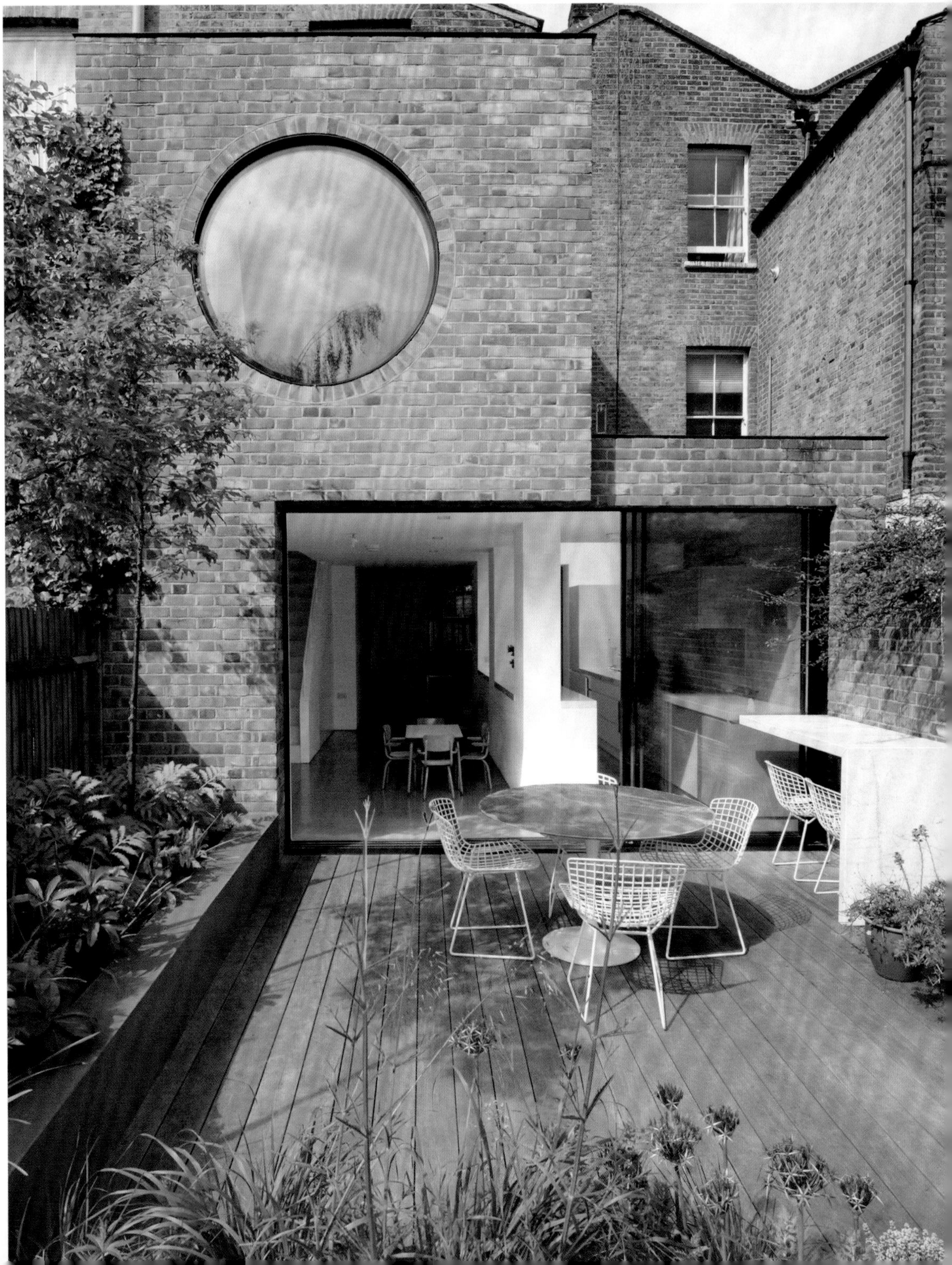

The renovation takes advantage of the generous spaces, stripping back unnecessary detailing to create spacious rooms, whilst the expansion makes the most of the removal of a conservatory building at the rear of the property, creating a sense of space.

La rénovation profite des volumes généreux, ayant éliminé ce qui était accessoire pour créer des pièces spacieuses, tandis que l'agrandissement tire profit de l'élimination d'une véranda à l'arrière de la propriété, créant une impression d'espace.

Der Umbau macht von den großzügigen Räumen Gebrauch und verzichtet auf unnötige Details, um geräumige Zimmer zu kreieren. Der Anbau nutzt die Beseitigung des Wintergartens an der Rückseite des Gebäudes optimal aus und lässt ein Gefühl von Raum entstehen.

La renovación se beneficia de los grandes espacios, quitando remates innecesarios para conseguir habitaciones espaciosas. Al mismo tiempo, la ampliación se aprovecha de la eliminación de un porche cerrado en la parte de atrás del terreno creando una sensación de espacio.

Original section

0   10 m

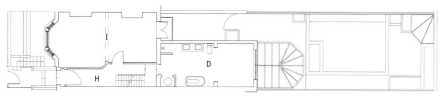

Original ground floor plan

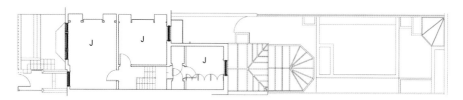

Original first floor plan

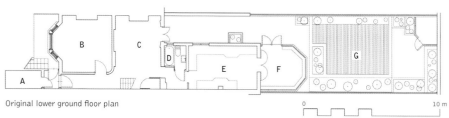

Original lower ground floor plan

0   10 m

A. Bike storage
B. Guest bedroom
C. Playroom
D. Bathroom
E. Kitchen
F. Dining room
G. Terrace
H. Entrance hall
I. Living room
J. Bedroom

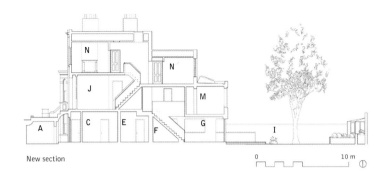

New section

0   10 m

New floor plan

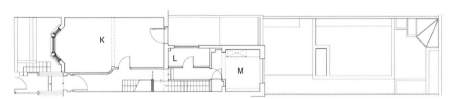

New ground floor plan

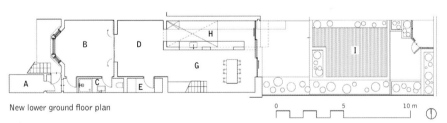

New lower ground floor plan

0   5   10 m

A. Bike storage   H. Kitchen
B. Guest bedroom   I. Terrace
C. En suite   J. Entrance hall
D. Playroom   K. Living room
E. Utility room   L. Storage room
F. Storage   M. Bathroom
G. Dining room   N. Bedroom

The rear façade has been carefully remodelled and punctuated with a circular window on the upper floor in reference to the pure geometric forms in the works of renowned British artists Barbara Hepworth and Ben Nicholson.

Die Rückfassade wurde sorgsam umgebaut und in Anlehnung an die puren geometrischen Formen in den Arbeiten der renommierten britischen Künstler Barbara Hepworth und Ben Nicholson im Obergeschoss mit einem runden Fenster versehen.

La façade arrière a été ré-agencée avec soin et relevée d'un oculus à l'étage supérieur en référence aux formes géométriques pures des travaux des artistes britanniques renommés Barbara Hepworth et Ben Nicholson.

La cuidada remodelación de la fachada trasera se ha acentuado con una ventana circular en el piso superior. Una referencia a las formas geométricas puras de los trabajos de los reconocidos artistas británicos Barbara Hepworth y Ben Nicholson.

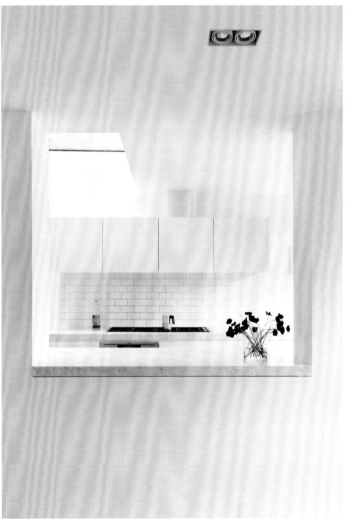

Clean lines are a predominant feature throughout the property. All faux stucco period elements have been stripped out, creating a minimalist backdrop for the display of mid-century furniture classics and a collection of contemporary art.

Das gesamte Gebäude zeichnet sich durch klare Linien aus. Alle Zierstuckelemente wurden entfernt, um eine minimalistische Kulisse für Mid-Century-Möbelklassiker und eine Sammlung zeitgenössischer Kunst entstehen zu lassen.

Les lignes épurées sont une caractéristique prédominante sur l'ensemble de la propriété. Tous les éléments d'époque en stuc ont été éliminés afin de créer un décor minimaliste pour des meubles classiques de la moitié du XXe siècle et une collection d'art contemporain.

La característica principal en toda la propiedad son las líneas puras. Se eliminaron los elementos de estuco, creando un telón minimalista para la muestra de muebles de mediados de siglo y una colección de arte contemporáneo.

The window is a central feature of the master bathroom. It provides expansive views of the lushly planted garden from the elegant freestanding claw foot bathtub.

Das Fenster ist ein zentraler Bestandteil des Master-Badezimmers. Von der eleganten frei stehenden Badewanne aus bietet es weite Ausblicke auf den üppig bepflanzten Garten.

L'oculus est un élément central de la salle d'eau principale. Elle offre des vues multiples sur le jardin luxuriant depuis l'élégante baignoire montée sur pieds de griffon.

La ventana del baño principal atrae todas las miradas. Desde la elegante bañera exenta con patas se disfruta de amplias vistas sobre la frondosa vegetación del jardín.

T19 HOUSE

An open and bright annex reorganises a townhouse

VUGHT, THE NETHERLANDS

TOTAL BUILDING AREA: 2314 sq ft – 215 m²
EXTENSION AREA: 215 sq ft – 20 m² // 9% of total area

A townhouse dating from 1905 was brought up to date to satisfy the contemporary lifestyle of its occupants. The initiative for the renovation of this historic house started with the wish of the client to have an eat-in kitchen directly connected with the backyard. The addition of a double-height open space at the rear of the existing house leads to the reconfiguration of the interior layout where lower and upper ground floors are interrelated and in direct contact with the backyard. A bold volume made of wood and glass stands out beside the brick house. Sophisticated detailing and a visual connection through the annex create synergy between old and new.

Une maison de ville datant de 1905 a été remise au goût du jour pour répondre au style de vie contemporain de ses occupants. L'initiative de la rénovation de cette maison historique est issue du souhait du client d'avoir une cuisine avec coin repas reliée directement à l'arrière-cour. L'ajout d'un espace ouvert en double hauteur à l'arrière de la maison existante entraîne la reconfiguration du plan intérieur où les étages inférieurs et supérieurs sont reliés entre eux et en contact direct avec l'arrière-cour. Un volume audacieux fait de bois et de verre se profile à côté de la maison en brique. Des détails raffinés et une connexion visuelle au travers de l'annexe créent une synergie entre l'ancien et le moderne.

Ein 1905 erbautes Townhouse wurde modernisiert, um dem zeitgemäßen Lebensstil der Bewohner gerecht zu werden. Die Initiative für die Renovierung dieses historischen Gebäudes begann mit dem Wunsch des Kunden nach einer Wohnküche, die mit dem hinter dem Haus liegenden Garten verbunden sein sollte. Der offen gehaltene Anbau mit doppelter Raumhöhe an der Rückseite des Gebäudes führt zu einer Umgestaltung der Aufteilung des Innenraums, in dem die untere und obere Etage miteinander verbunden sind und direkten Kontakt zum Garten haben. Der prägnante Anbau aus Holz und Glas sticht neben dem Backsteinhaus hervor. Anspruchsvolle Details und eine visuelle Verbindung durch den Anbau lassen eine Synergie zwischen Alt und Neu entstehen.

Una casa adosada de 1905 se modernizó para satisfacer el actual estilo de vida de sus ocupantes. La iniciativa de remodelación de esta vivienda histórica comenzó con el deseo del cliente de tener una cocina con *office* conectada directamente con el jardín. Al sumarle en la parte de atrás de la casa un espacio abierto de doble altura, cambió la configuración de toda la vivienda, en la que ahora la planta baja y el semisótano están relacionados y en contacto directo con el jardín. Un volumen audaz de madera y cristal destaca tras la casa de ladrillo. Detalles elegantes y la conexión visual a través del anexo crean una sinergia entre lo nuevo y lo antiguo.

In the former situation, the basement was used as storage. Daylight came in muted because of its low ceiling height and an obscure rear façade.

Dans la configuration précédente, le sous-sol servait de rangement. La lumière du jour était diffuse à cause de la hauteur de plafond limitée et de l'obscure façade arrière de la maison.

Zuvor wurde das Tiefparterre als Lagerraum genutzt. Aufgrund der niedrigen Raumhöhe und der dunklen Fassade an der Rückseite trat nur gedämpftes Licht ein.

Antes de la renovación, el sótano se usaba como almacén. La baja altura del techo y la oscura fachada trasera impedían que apenas entrase luz natural.

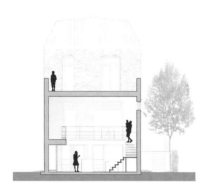

New building sections

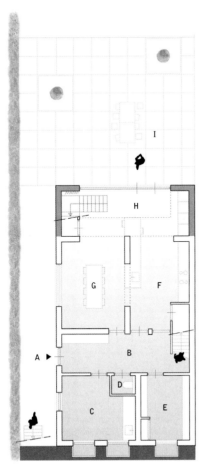

New ground floor plan

New second floor plan

A. Entrance
B. Service entrance
C. Laundry room
D. WC room
E. Storage room
F. Kitchen
G. Dining room
H. Annex
I. Garden
J. Hall
K. Living room
L. Hallway
M. Dining room

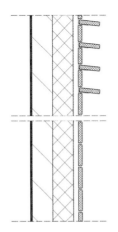

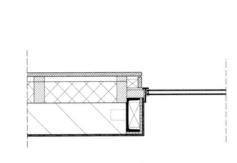

Cladding details

Inside, the combination of white walls, warm grey flooring and oak cabinets provides an intimate atmosphere, which naturally adds to the existing historic townhouse. The staircase in the double height space is a sculptural element made of folded steel sheet.

Im Inneren sorgt die Kombination von weißen Wänden, warmen grauen Böden und Eichenschränken für eine gemütliche Atmosphäre, die das Flair des historischen Townhouses unterstreicht. Die Treppe in dem Raum mit doppelter Raumhöhe ist ein skulpturales Element aus gefaltetem Stahlblech.

À l'intérieur, la combinaison de murs blancs, de sols d'un gris chaleureux et de placards en chêne dégage une ambiance intimiste qui contribue naturellement à la maison existante. L'escalier de l'espace en double hauteur est un élément sculptural fait de tôle d'acier façonnée.

Dentro, la combinación de paredes blancas, suelo de color gris cálido y armarios de roble proporciona una atmósfera íntima que se integra naturalmente con el adosado histórico existente. La escalera en el espacio a doble altura es un elemento arquitectónico hecho de láminas de acero doblado.

The use of black steel in the interior and exterior enhances the historic character of the house. Detailing and colour scheme are contemporary, avoiding rivalry with the existing classical mouldings on doors, walls and ceilings.

Die Verwendung von schwarzem Stahl innen und außen betont den historischen Charakter des Hauses. Die Details und die Farbgebung sind zeitgenössisch und lassen keine Rivalität zu den bestehenden klassischen Stuckarbeiten an Türen, Wänden und Decken entstehen.

L'usage d'acier noir à l'intérieur et à l'extérieur fait ressortir le caractère historique de la maison. Les décors et le jeu des couleurs sont contemporains sans rivaliser avec les moulages classiques d'origine sur les portes, les murs et les plafonds.

El uso de acero negro en el interior y exterior realza el carácter histórico de la vivienda. Los remates y la paleta de colores que se han utilizado son contemporáneos, evitando rivalizar con los acabados clásicos presentes en puertas, paredes y techos.

EXTENSION VUGHT
Transformation of a low and dark basement

VUGHT, THE NETHERLANDS

TOTAL BUILDING AREA: 775 sq ft – 72 m²
EXTENSION AREA: 215 sq ft – 20 m² // 28% of total area

This extending renovation of an existing townhouse was necessary to satisfy the needs of a large family. With an upper ground floor above street level and a garden at the rear of the property sunken at basement level, the house suffered from a lack of easy access between the living areas and the exterior. Whilst the basement had a low ceiling — and for this reason it was only used for storage —, it offered the opportunity and the potential for the creation of a spacious living area with direct access to the garden. By doing this, the ground floor would lend itself for a reorganization to accommodate other spatial needs of the family.

Cette rénovation avec extension d'une maison de ville existante était nécessaire pour répondre aux besoins d'une grande famille. Avec un entresol au-dessus du niveau de la rue et un jardin à l'arrière de la propriété en contrebas, au niveau du sous-sol, la maison pâtissait d'un manque d'accessibilité entre les pièces à vivre et l'extérieur. Tout en ayant un plafond bas — c'est pour cette raison qu'il n'était utilisé que pour le rangement —, le sous-sol offrait la possibilité et le potentiel de création d'une zone spacieuse à vivre en accès direct avec le jardin. Avec cette transformation, le rez-de-chaussée pouvait se prêter à une réorganisation pouvant répondre à d'autres besoins de la famille au niveau de l'espace.

Der Umbau war erforderlich, um den Bedürfnissen einer großen Familien zu entsprechen. Mit einem Hochparterre über Straßenhöhe und einem Garten auf Höhe des Tiefparterres hinter dem Haus fehlte ein leichter Zugang zwischen den Wohnbereichen und dem Außenbereich. Obwohl das Tiefparterre eine niedrige Decke hatte – und aus diesem Grund nur als Lagerraum genutzt wurde –, bot es die Möglichkeit und das Potenzial, einen geräumigen Wohnbereich mit direktem Gartenzugang zu kreieren. So würde sich das Erdgeschoss für eine Umstrukturierung anbieten, um die weiteren räumlichen Bedürfnisse der Familie zu erfüllen.

La gran familia que habitaba esta casa adosada necesitaba una ampliación de la misma. El desnivel del terreno –la planta baja está al nivel de la calle, mientras que el sótano se encuentra al nivel del jardín trasero– impedía una conexión directa entre la zona de vida y el exterior. Por su baja altura, el sótano solo se usaba para almacenaje. Sin embargo, tenía potencial para transformarse en una zona común espaciosa con acceso directo al jardín. Con este cambio, la planta baja se reorganizaría para albergar otras zonas necesarias para la familia.

BUROKOEK

The excavation of the basement to increase its ceiling height made possible to move the kitchen, living room and dining room—originally on the ground floor—down to the garden level. The existing garden staircase was internalized in a new window frame.

L'excavation du sous-sol pour augmenter la hauteur de plafond a permis de déplacer la cuisine, le séjour et la salle-à-manger – autrefois au rez-de-chaussée – au niveau du jardin. L'ancien escalier du jardin a été intégré dans un nouvel encadrement de fenêtre.

Der Ausbau des Tiefparterres zur Erweiterung der Deckenhöhe ermöglichte es, die Küche, das Wohn- und Esszimmer – ursprünglich im Erdgeschoss – unten im Gartengeschoss unterzubringen. Die bestehende Gartentreppe wurde in einem neuen Fensterstock in den Innenraum integriert.

La excavación del sótano para incrementar la altura del techo hizo posible trasladar la cocina, la sala de estar y el comedor –originalmente en la planta baja– al nivel del jardín. La escalera existente del jardín se incluyó en la ampliación de cristal.

Computer generated rendering. Exterior view of extension

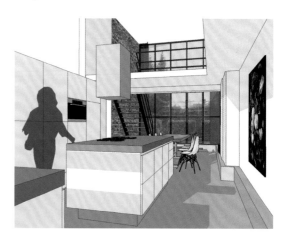

Computer generated rendering. Interior view of extension

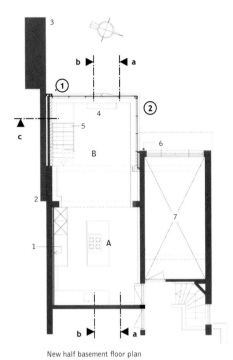

New half basement floor plan

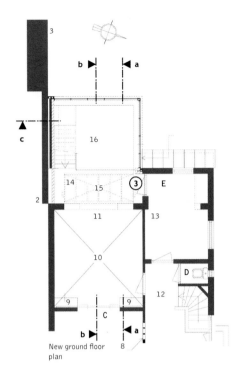

New ground floor plan

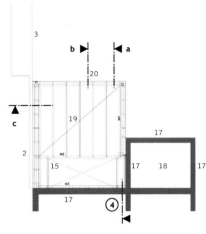

Framing plan

A. Kitchen
B. Dining area
C. Living area
D. WC room
E. Office

1. New double wall to mitigate moisture problem through existing exterior wall
2. Adjacent party wall

3. Adjacent building
4. New oak step
5. Existing steel staircase with new oak treads
6. Downspout
7. Room remains unchanged
8. Doorway between living room and hallway sealed with plasterboard and stucco finish
9. Cabinet

10. Living room remains unchanged
11. Opening frame removed. Lintel remains. New stone threshold
12. Hall remains unchanged
13. Ceiling is maintained. Wall tiles are removed. Walls are plastered smooth
14. Existing landing remains unchanged
15. Skylight above
16. Open to below
17. Existing wall

18. Existing balcony
19. 46 x 146 beams
20. To existing sewer line 46 x 146 beams + 18 mm plywood decking

sk1 = Steel column 90 x 90 x 6
sb1 = HE120A steel beam + steel column
sb2 = HE140A steel beam
sb3 = 100 x 100 x 10 steel angle

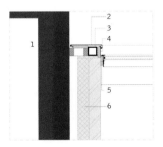

Detail 1

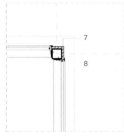

Detail 2

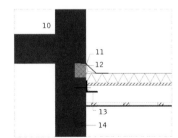

Detail 3

Detail 4

1. Adjacent property
2. Clip mounting zinc metal sheet
3. 80 x 80 tube
4. Black zinc
5. 20 mm wood block
6. 100 mm insulation
7. 12 mm plywood + Sendzimir sheet

8. Steel column 90 x 90 x 6 mm
9. 1.5 mm Sendzimir sheet
10. Existing floor slab
11. Metal flashing
12. Cellular concrete (thermal bridge break)
13. 100 x 100 x 10 mm steel angle
14. Exposed original masonry wall

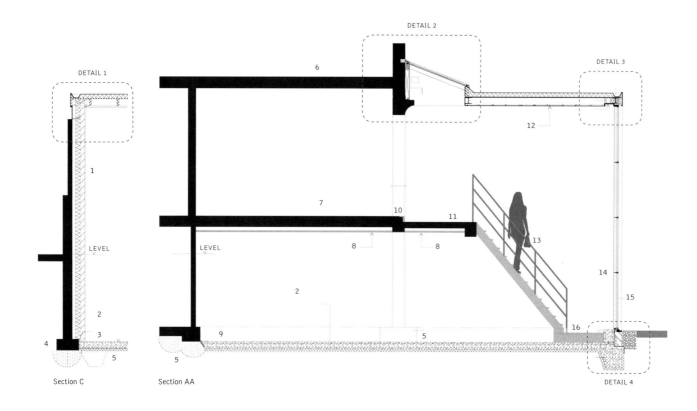

DETAIL 1

DETAIL 2

DETAIL 3

DETAIL 4

Section C

Section AA

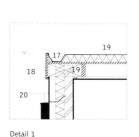

Detail 1

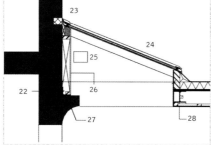

Detail 2

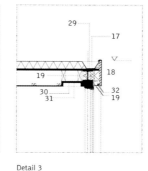

Detail 3

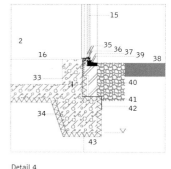

Detail 4

1. Partition wall
   - Existing party wall
   - Limestone
   - 50 mm insulation
   - Brick wall (used brick)
2. Half basement floor
   - 150 mm concrete slab (with radiant heat)
   - 75 mm Floormate 500 insulation board
   - PE waterproofing membrane
   - Compacted sand bed
3. Thermal bridge break
4. Foundation depth of existing party wall unknown

5. Existing foundation to remain untouched
6. Second floor
   Existing floor and lintels unchanged
7. Ground floor
   Existing floor and lintels unchanged
8. Plasterboard ceiling, smooth plaster finish
9. New foundation connected to existing with chemical anchors
10. New hardwood threshold
11. Existing landing and lintels unchanged

12. Acoustic ceiling, smooth finish
13. Steel staircase with new oak treads
14. Door opening height 2300 mm min.
15. Window details by manufacturer
16. Wooden platform
17. Rain gutter
18. 20 mm plywood fascia + zinc sheet
19. Wood blocking
20. Stucco reveal and metal flashing
21. Flat roof detail
    - Bituminous roofing membrane
    - 80 mm min. rigid foam insulation
    - 18 mm plywood roof decking
    - 46 x 146 mm beam

   - 20 mm battens
   - Acoustic ceiling
22. 100 x 100 x 10 steel angle anchored to wall
23. Lead and cellular concrete (thermal bridge break)
24. Prefabricated skylight and support beams, painted white
25. Ventilation grill
26. Plasterboard
    45 x 90 furring
    10 mm plaster and stucco
27. Existing concrete lintel
28. HE140A beam
29. HE120A beam

30. 18 mm plywood
31. 50 x 200 ceiling cove
32. Black zinc
33. Rebar dia. 6-300
34. Rebar dia. 8-300
35. Safety glass
36. 20 mm plywood
37. Metal profile
38. Ground
39. Stone threshold
40. Gravel bed to prevent splashing
41. Cellular concrete (thermal bridge break)
42. Metal flashing
43. Floormate 500

In this living room-style kitchen, old and new come together symbiotically by, among other things, juxtaposing the old exposed bricks with the new concrete flooring, white oak woodwork, and steel railings and window frames.

In dieser Wohnküche treffen Alt und Neu symbiotisch aufeinander, unter anderem durch die Nebeneinanderstellung von dem alten freigelegten Mauerwerk mit dem neuen Betonboden, den weißen Eichenholzarbeiten, dem Stahlgeländer und den Stahlfensterrahmen.

Dans cette cuisine salle-à-manger, l'ancien et le nouveau se retrouvent associés en symbiose par, entre autres choses, la juxtaposition des anciens parements de briques avec le nouveau sol de béton, des boiseries en chêne blanc, et des balustrades et cadres de fenêtres en acier.

En este salón con cocina abierta, lo antiguo y lo nuevo se unen y contrastan: los antiguos ladrillos vistos con el suelo nuevo de cemento; los remates de madera de roble blanca con las barandillas de acero y los marcos de las ventanas.

THE GLASS HOUSE

Bright space. Bridging the gap

LONDON, UNITED KINGDOM

TOTAL BUILDING AREA: 4200 sq ft – 390 m^2
EXTENSION AREA: 580 sq ft – 54 m^2 // 14% of total area

The glass extension reinvents the feel and atmosphere of the once dark and cramped servant's quarters of a large manor house, all within the rich historical context of the site. The concept was to provide a clean and light architectural intervention alongside the traditional shell of the building. A clearly defined spatial organization was designed to contrast the bright and open communal spaces in the addition to the more subtle and secluded retreat spaces in the old house. In all, the modern renovation and extension create a light, airy and open living environment bursting with traditional values, contemporary style and innovative design.

L'extension vitrée réinvente la sensation et l'atmosphère des quartiers des domestiques d'une grande maison de maître, autrefois sombres et exigus, tout en préservant le riche contexte historique du site. Une organisation spatiale clairement définie a été conçue pour faire contraster les espaces communaux lumineux et ouverts dans leur ajout à ceux, plus subtils et retirés, de la vieille maison. Partout, la rénovation moderne et l'extension créent un environnement vital lumineux, aéré et ouvert où abondent valeurs traditionnelles, style contemporain et design novateur.

Der Anbau aus Glas erfindet das einst dunkle und beengte Dienstbotenquartier eines großen Herrenhauses im historischen Kontext des Grundstücks neu. Das Konzept bestand darin, entlang dem traditionellen Mauerwerk des Gebäudes einen leichten architektonischen Eingriff vorzunehmen. Es wurde eine klare räumliche Anordnung festgelegt, um die hellen und offenen Gemeinschaftsräume im Anbau von den dezenteren und abgeschiedeneren Rückzugsräumen im alten Haus abzugrenzen. Insgesamt sorgen die moderne Renovierung und der Anbau für eine helle, lichtdurchflutete und offene Wohnumgebung, die sich durch traditionelle Werte, einen zeitgenössischen Stil und ein innovatives Design auszeichnet.

La ampliación de cristal reinventa la sensación y la atmósfera de las anteriormente oscuras y estrechas estancias de los sirvientes en la gran casa, todo dentro del rico contexto histórico del lugar. El concepto consistía en dar un toque arquitectónico puro y luminoso junto a la fachada tradicional del edificio. Se diseñó una organización espacial claramente definida para contrastar, por un lado, los espacios comunes luminosos y abiertos ubicados en la ampliación y, por otro, los espacios privados más sutiles y aislados que se albergan en la antigua casa. En resumen, la moderna renovación y ampliación crean un entorno vital luminoso, espacioso y abierto rebosante de valores tradicionales, estilo contemporáneo y diseño innovador.

The existing layout was clarified. Vertical voids were cut through the house to unite the cellar, the ground and first floors and redirect the flow of the house to naturally draw the user toward the new glass space.

Le plan d'origine a été épuré. Des vides verticaux ont été pratiqués à divers endroits de la maison pour relier la cave, le rez-de-chaussée et le premier étage et rediriger la circulation de la maison pour attirer l'usager vers le nouvel espace vitré.

Der bestehende Grundriss wurde klarer gestaltet. Es wurden vertikale Räume in das Haus eingefügt, die den Keller, das Erdgeschoss und die Obergeschosse miteinander verbinden und den Fluss des Hauses umlenken, um die Bewohner in Richtung des neuen Glasraumes zu führen.

El plano existente se depuró. Se crearon espacios verticales para unir el sótano con la planta baja y la primera. Esta disposición también redirige el flujo de la casa y atrae al habitante de forma natural hacia el nuevo espacio de cristal.

New southeast elevation

New section BB

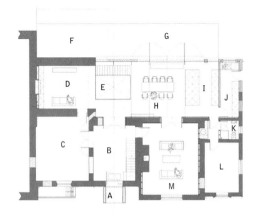

New ground floor plan

New first floor plan

A. Entrance porch
B. Entrance hall
C. Formal dining room
D. Living area
E. Void
F. Existing conservatory
G. Patio
H. Dining area
I. Kitchen
J. Utility room
K. Powder room
L. Study/guestroom
M. Formal lounge
N. Landing
O. Bedroom
P. Bathroom
Q. Laundry room
R. En suite bathroom
S. Dressing area
T. Master bedroom

This light and spacious frameless glass structure houses the open-plan kitchen, living and dining areas. As a contrast to the extension, the formal lounge, study and dining room have a more sheltered nature.

Der helle und geräumige rahmenlose Glasbau beherbergt einen offenen Raum, in dem sich Küche, Wohn- und Essbereich befinden. Als Kontrast zum Anbau haben das repräsentative Wohnzimmer, das Arbeits- und das Esszimmer einen geschützteren Charakter.

Cette structure de verre à cadre masqué, lumineuse et spacieuse, accueille la cuisine ouverte, la salle-à-manger et le séjour. En contraste avec l'extension, le salon plus formel, le bureau et la salle-à-manger sont davantage fermés sur eux-mêmes.

Esta amplia y luminosa estructura de cristal alberga una cocina abierta, zona de día y comedor. Como contraste a la ampliación, el salón, el estudio y el comedor tienen un carácter más protegido.

Whilst still retaining a subtle street appearance, the finished property is completely transformed from its previous gloomy nature. Strategically placed skylights and large windows flood the interior with light and open it to the garden.

Auch wenn das fertiggestellte Gebäude ein dezentes Äußeres bewahrt hat, hat es sich verglichen mit seinem vorherigen düsteren Charakter komplett gewandelt. Strategisch platzierte Oberlichter und große Fenster überfluten den Innenraum mit Licht und öffnen ihn zum Garten.

Tout en conservant son aspect discret, la propriété terminée a complètement perdu de son aspect morose. Des fenêtres de toit et de grandes ouvertures stratégiquement placées inondent l'intérieur de lumière et l'ouvrent sur le jardin.

Pese a que sigue conservando su aspecto sutil desde la calle, la vivienda se transforma por completo desde su anterior naturaleza sombría. Tragaluces estratégicamente colocados y grandes ventanales inundan el interior de luz y la abren al jardín.

CAMPDEN GROVE

Kensington Townhouse

LONDON, UNITED KINGDOM

TOTAL BUILDING AREA: 3233 sq ft – 300 m²
EXTENSION AREA: 861 sq ft – 80 m² // 27% of total area

A traditional and slightly tired townhouse was brought back to life with a sensible renovation and contemporary expansion to reflect the needs of the client's young family, whilst maintaining the classical character of the building. The client wanted to add space with a basement and closet wing extension to create an additional bedroom, a gym, and cinema room. Not only did this provide an opportunity to restructure the property and create larger interconnected spaces, but also to open the interior to a compact garden and give a much greater sense of space.

Une maison de ville traditionnelle et un peu défraîchie a été revigorée par une rénovation judicieuse et une extension contemporaine qui reflètent les besoins de la jeune famille du client tout en maintenant le caractère classique du bâtiment. L'occupant voulait avoir davantage d'espace par le biais d'un sous-sol et d'une extension à l'arrière de la maison pour créer une chambre supplémentaire, une salle de gym, et une salle de cinéma. Cette initiative a non seulement représenté une opportunité de restructurer la propriété et de créer des espaces plus généreux, reliés entre eux, mais aussi d'ouvrir l'intérieur sur un jardin compact et d'accentuer l'impression d'espace.

Ein traditionelles und leicht ermüdetes Townhouse wurde mit einer angemessenen Renovierung und einem zeitgenössischen Anbau wieder zum Leben erweckt, um den Bedürfnissen der jungen Familie des Kunden zu entsprechen, wobei der klassische Charakter des Gebäudes bewahrt wurde. Der Kunde wünschte sich mehr Platz durch eine Erweiterung des Tiefparterres und einen Anbau an der Rückseite, um ein zusätzliches Schlafzimmer, einen Fitness- und einen Kinoraum einzurichten. Dadurch bot sich nicht nur die Gelegenheit, das Gebäude neu zu strukturieren und miteinander verbundene Räume entstehen zu lassen, sondern es war auch möglich, die Innenräume zu dem kompakten Garten zu öffnen und dem Haus ein viel großzügigeres Raumgefühl zu verleihen.

Una casa adosada tradicional y ligeramente destartalada volvió a brillar con una renovación apropiada y una ampliación contemporánea que refleja las necesidades de la joven familia del cliente, a la vez que mantiene el carácter clásico del edificio. El cliente quería aumentar espacio con un sótano y una extensión en la parte de atrás de la casa para crear un dormitorio adicional, un gimnasio y una sala de cine. Además de proporcionar una oportunidad para reestructurar la propiedad y crear espacios interconectados más amplios, este cambio también permitió abrir el interior a un pequeño jardín y dar mayor sensación de espacio.

TIGG + COLL ARCHITECTS

The original home was already substantial, but the split levels between a closet wing and main house, and the lack of light to the lower ground floor meant that it felt constrained and dingy.

La maison d'origine était déjà de taille, mais de par les différences de niveau entre l'aile arrière et la maison principale, et le manque de lumière dans le deuxième sous-sol, elle donnait l'impression d'être étriquée et terne.

Das ursprüngliche Haus war bereits beachtlich, aber durch die unterbrochenen Ebenen zwischen Anbau und Haupthaus und das fehlende Licht im Tiefparterre wirkte es eng und düster.

La vivienda original ya era amplia, pero parecía constreñida y lóbrega, por la diferencia de nivel entre la extensión trasera y la casa principal y la falta de luz en el semisótano.

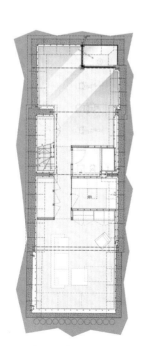

New basement floor plan

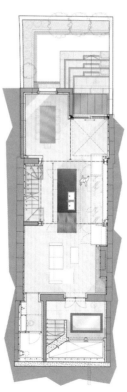

New lower ground floor plan

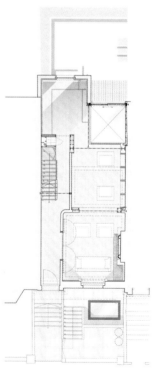

New ground floor plan

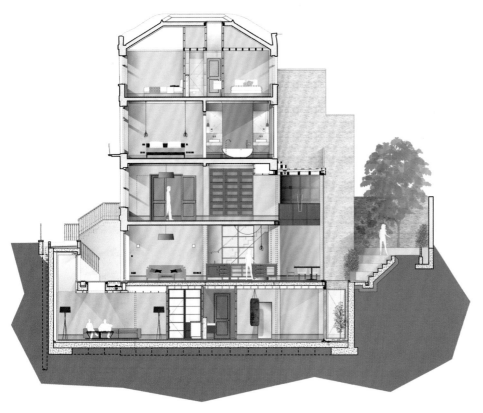

New building section

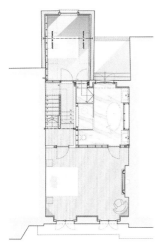

New first floor plan

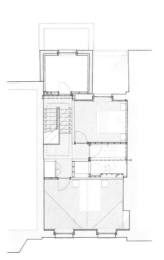

New second floor plan

The basement, lower and upper ground floors are open to a small terraced garden at the back of the property. This was achieved by installing six-meter-tall glazed sliding doors to a double-height void between the lower and raised ground floors.

Das Tief- und das Hochparterre sowie das Obergeschoss öffnen sich zu einem kleinen Terrassengarten an der Rückseite. Dies wurde durch sechs Meter hohe Schiebetüren aus Glas erreicht, die in einem Hohlraum mit doppelter Raumhöhe zwischen Tief- und Hochparterre eingesetzt wurden.

Les premier et deuxième sous-sols sont ouverts sur un petit jardin en terrasse à l'arrière de la propriété. Cet effet a été atteint grâce à l'installation de coulissants vitrés de six mètres de haut dans un espace en double hauteur entre les deux sous-sols.

El sótano, el semisótano y la planta baja están abiertos a un pequeño jardín en terrazas en la parte de atrás de la propiedad. Se consiguió instalando una puerta deslizante de cristal de seis metros de alto en un vacío a doble altura, entre el semisótano y la planta principal.

The basement excavation helped maximize the floor-to-ceiling height and natural light. This turned what had been a dark an unwelcoming series of small rooms into a bright and inviting open-plan kitchen, dining and family room.

Der Ausbau des Untergeschosses maximierte die gesamte Raumhöhe und den Lichteinfall. So wurde aus einer Reihe dunkler und unfreundlicher kleiner Räume ein heller und einladender offener Familienraum mit Küche und Essbereich.

L'excavation de la cave a permis d'optimiser la hauteur sous plafond et la lumière naturelle. Ainsi ce qui était une série sombre et peu engageante de petites pièces a été transformé en cuisine ouverte, salle-à-manger et pièce à vivre lumineuses et accueillantes.

La excavación en el sótano ayudó a maximizar la altura de suelo a techo y la luz natural. Esto convirtió lo que habían sido una serie de habitaciones poco atractivas en un espacio abierto luminoso y acogedor que incluía la cocina, el comedor y la zona de estar.

The client was keen to maintain the traditional character of the property across the upper three storeys, so a more restrained and classical approach was adopted for these.

Der Kunde wollte den traditionellen Charakter des Gebäudes auf den oberen drei Etagen beibehalten. Aus diesem Grund wurde für diese Ebenen ein Ansatz gewählt, der zurückhaltender und klassischer ist.

Le client tenant à préserver le caractère traditionnel de la propriété pour les trois étages supérieurs, une approche plus mesurée et plus classique y a été adoptée.

El cliente deseaba mantener el carácter tradicional de la vivienda en las tres plantas superiores, por lo que en estas se adaptó un enfoque más clásico y contenido.

JJ HOUSE
When Judd met Eames

LONDON, UNITED KINGDOM

TOTAL BUILDING AREA: 1507 sq ft – 140 m²
EXTENSION AREA: 538 sq ft – 50 m² // 36% of total area

A house dated from the 1830's only accepted a discreet and elegant extension form a conservation point of view. This extension led to a major interior reconfiguration.
A new glass box, sunken below ground level against a vertical garden, houses a dining area, whilst the opening up of the existing house interior enables the flow of natural light. The old external vaults have been converted into an herb garden and a wine storage. A new mansard roof extension provides space for an additional master bedroom and en suite bathroom, accessed through a sliding wooden screen.

Pour des raisons de conservation du patrimoine, cette maison datant des années 1930 ne pouvait recevoir qu'une extension discrète et élégante. Celle-ci a entraîné une reconfiguration majeure à l'intérieur du bâtiment.
Un nouveau module en verre, en contrebas par rapport au niveau du sol, appuyé contre un jardin vertical, accueille un coin repas, tandis que l'ouverture de l'intérieur de la maison existante permet la circulation de lumière naturelle. Les anciennes voûtes extérieures ont été converties en jardin aromatique et cave-à-vin. Une nouvelle extension mansardée offre de l'espace pour une suite parentale supplémentaire et salle d'eau adjacente, accessible par un panneau coulissant en bois.

Ein Haus aus dem Jahr 1830 konnte aus Denkmalschutzgründen nur mit einer dezenten und eleganten Erweiterung versehen werden. Diese Erweiterung führte zu einer großen Umgestaltung des Innenbereichs.
In einem neuen Glaskastenbau, der unterhalb der Erdgeschossebene an einem vertikalen Garten liegt, ist ein Essbereich untergebracht. Durch die Öffnung des Innenraums des bestehenden Hauses wird dieser mit Licht durchflutet. Die alten Außengewölbe wurden zu einem Kräutergarten und Weinlager umfunktioniert. Durch eine Mansardendacherweiterung wurde Platz für ein zusätzliches Hauptschlafzimmer und ein dazugehöriges Badezimmer geschaffen, das durch eine Schiebewand aus Holz vom Schlafzimmer getrennt ist.

Para conservar intacta esta casa construida en la década de 1830 solo se podía hacer una ampliación discreta y elegante. Esta ha provocado una reconfiguración del espacio interior.
Una nueva caja de cristal, hundida bajo el nivel del terreno contra un jardín vertical, alberga el comedor a la vez que abre el espacio interior y permite que fluya la luz natural. Las antiguas bóvedas exteriores se han convertido en un jardín de hierbas y una bodega. Una ampliación abuhardillada en el tejado genera espacio para otro dormitorio principal con baño, al que se accede a través de una puerta deslizante realizada en madera, que llega de suelo a techo.

SPACE GROUP OF ARCHITECTS

Whilst historical features have been discovered and maintained, they now sit in stark contrast with the modern interior design. But it is the discrete technical interventions that preserve this building and enable a suitable use.

Les aspects historiques ayant été découverts et préservés, ils contrastent maintenant de façon saisissante avec le design intérieur moderne. Mais ce sont les discrètes interventions techniques qui conservent ce bâtiment et en permettent une utilisation correcte.

Historische Merkmale wurden entdeckt und bewahrt und bilden jetzt einen deutlichen Kontrast zu der modernen Innenarchitktur. Aber es sind die dezenten technischen Maßnahmen, die dieses Gebäude bewahren und seine angemessene Nutzung sicherstellen.

A primera vista, destaca el contraste entre las características históricas de la vivienda descubiertas y conservadas en esta remodelación y el moderno diseño interior. Sin embargo, son las discretas incorporaciones técnicas las que preservan esta casa y permiten su uso.

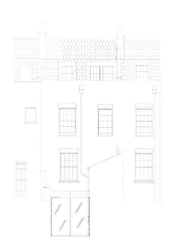

New rear elevation

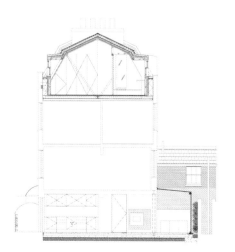
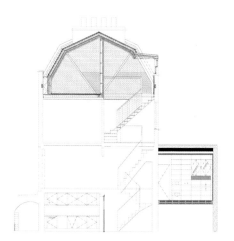

New building sections

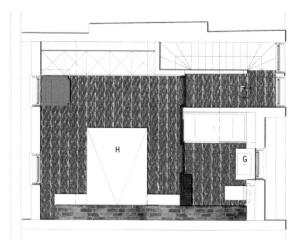

New second floor plan

A. Vestibule
B. Kitchen
C. Vaults
D. Reading area
E. Dining area
F. Hallway
G. Master bathroom
H. Master bedroom

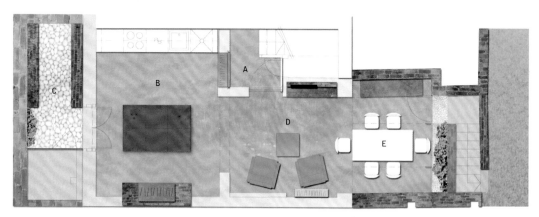

New ground floor plan

At the new top floor, some existing party walls have been left exposed, whilst others have been lined. The new roof structure has also been left exposed in order to blur the boundaries between the new and the found space.

Im neuen Obergeschoss wurden einige der bestehenden Außenwände freigelegt, während andere verkleidet wurden. Auch die neue Dachstruktur wurde freigelegt, um die Grenzen zwischen dem neuen und dem vorgefundenen Raum zu verwischen.

Au niveau de l'actuel dernier étage, certains murs mitoyens existants ont été laissés découverts tandis que d'autres ont été doublés. La nouvelle charpente a également été laissée apparente pour estomper les limites entre le nouvel espace et l'original.

En el nuevo espacio del piso superior, algunos muros ya existentes se han dejado al descubierto y otros se han recubierto. No se ha tapado la nueva estructura del tejado para difuminar las fronteras entre el espacio nuevo y el antiguo.

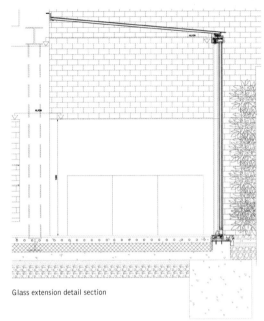

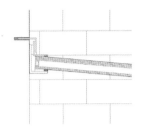

Top detail. Glass roof

Glass extension detail section

New insulated and waterproofed floor build-up:
- 14 mm x 1200 mm x 300 mm recycled concrete floor boards CF01 by Concreate; colour: natural; Woca oil finish;
- on 3 mm rubber granulate adhesive bed by Concreate.
- 75 mm screed with underfloor heating.
- Separating layer of building paper to BS 1521: 1972 (1994), Grade
- B1F or polythene sheet (not less than 125 micron / 500 gauge)
- 100 mm Kingspan Kooltherm K3 floorboard
- DPM. Min. 1200 g Blue 1200 by NDC or similar approved
- 150 mm concrete slab
- 50 mm blinding
- 150 mm compressed hardcore

External floor:
- Bed of stone pebbles
- 75 mm screed
- 50 mm blinding
- 150 mm compressed hardcore

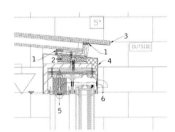

Top detail. Door

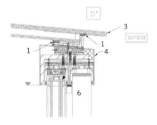

Top detail. Fixed glazed unit

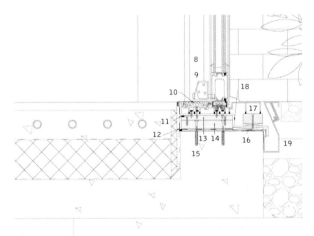

Bottom detail. Door

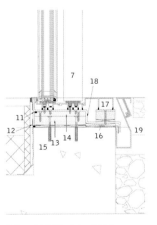

Bottom detail. Fixed glazed detail

1. Mastic seal
2. HDPE
3. Chamfered and polished edge
4. Aluminium cover pressing on 25 mm plywood by others
5. Hit and miss vent
6. Trickle vent
7. End profile of sliding door
8. End profile of fixed light
9. Secondary lock
10. Insulation
11. Butyl tape
12. Mastic seal between DPC's
13. 22 mm plywood
14. 12 mm plywood
15. 2.5" long No. 10 C/sk Rawlplug wood screws
16. DPM to overlap DPM on drain
17. 2 m x 25 x 50mm nylon packers at 150 cm
18. 4 mm aluminium levelling plate silicone sealed to the structure at both ends
19. "Hepworth" drain

Rich materials such as clay render, exposed brickwork, fair-faced concrete, exposed structural steel, matt white mosaic tiles, and copper ironmongery, sit comfortably next to Charles Eames, Poul Henningsen, and Dieter Rams.

Edle Materialien, wie Lehmputz, freiliegendes Mauerwerk, Sichtbeton, freiliegender Baustahl, mattweiße Mosaikfliesen und Kupferdetails sind im Einklang mit Charles Eames, Poul Henningsen und Dieter Rams.

De superbes matériaux tels que des enduits d'argile, briques apparentes, bétons bruts, structures en acier apparentes, dalles de mosaïque blanc mat, et accessoires en cuivre trouvent naturellement leur place auprès de Charles Eames, Poul Henningsen, et Dieter Rams.

Materiales ricos —enlucido de arcilla, ladrillo y hormigón visto, estructuras de acero a la vista, azulejos tipo mosaico en blanco mate y herrajes en cobre— combinan perfectamente con diseños de Charles Earnes, Poul Henningsen y Dieter Rams.

Donald Judd and Dan Flavin have a strong influence on some of the minimalist details, which can be found throughout the house. One can also sense a deliberate Japanese aura, which is an homage to one of the client's childhood.

Donald Judd und Dan Flavin haben einen starken Einfluss auf einige minimalistische Details, die überall im Haus anzufinden sind. Zudem ist ein gewolltes japanisches Flair wahrnehmbar – eine Hommage an die Kindheit von einem der Kunden.

Donald Judd et Dan Flavin ont une forte influence sur certains des détails minimalistes qui se trouvent partout dans la maison. Il y règne également une ambiance japonaise étudiée, en hommage à l'enfance de l'un des clients.

Algunos de los detalles minimalistas que pueden encontrarse por toda la vivienda tienen una gran influencia de Donald Judd y Dan Flavin. También puede sentirse una deliberada aura japonesa, homenaje a la infancia de uno de los clientes.

CAMPANULES

Opening up to the Garden

BRUSSELS, BELGIUM

TOTAL BUILDING AREA: 2013 sq ft – 187 m^2
EXTENSION AREA: 108 sq ft – 10 m^2 // 5,5% of total area

The dramatic extension of an urban house opens up the entire rear elevation to the garden. It also increases the area of the kitchen and dining area, whilst keeping them in their original location. Using an architectural expression that counterpoints the existing style, the coexistence between old and new is emphasised. The use of steel gives the new house a sharp look, whilst Corten steel ties the house to the garden, conceptually referring to the pass of time and seasons expressed by the changes in colour and texture of the vegetation.

Dans cette impressionnante extension d'une maison de ville, la totalité de l'élévation arrière ouvre sur le jardin. La surface du coin cuisine-salle-à-manger y est également augmentée tout en en conservant l'implantation d'origine. Par le biais d'une expression architecturale en contrepoint au style existant, la coexistence entre l'ancien et le nouveau se trouve accentuée. L'usage de l'acier confère à la nouvelle maison une belle esthétique, tandis que l'acier Corten relie la maison au jardin, en faisant référence conceptuellement au passage du temps et des saisons exprimé par les changements de couleur et de texture de la végétation.

Durch den spektakulären Anbau eines städtischen Hauses wird die gesamte Rückseite zum Garten geöffnet. Außerdem wird der Küchen- und Essbereich, der an seinem ursprünglichen Standort verbleibt, vergrößert. Der verwendete architektonische Ausdruck ist ein Kontrapunkt zum bestehenden Stil, sodass die Koexistenz von Alt und Neu betont wird. Die Verwendung von Stahl verleiht dem neuen Haus ein prägnantes Aussehen und gleichzeitig schafft der Cortenstahl eine Verbindung zwischen Haus und Garten. Dies ist eine konzeptuelle Bezugnahme auf den Verlauf der Zeit und der Jahreszeiten, der sich durch Änderungen der Farbe und Beschaffenheit der Vegetation ausdrückt.

La notable extensión de una casa urbana abre el alzado trasero al jardín. También aumenta el espacio de la cocina y del comedor, aunque conservan el mismo emplazamiento. Se enfatiza la coexistencia de lo nuevo y lo antiguo usando una expresión arquitectónica de contrapunto con el estilo existente. El uso del acero confiere a la nueva vivienda elegancia a la vez que el acero Corten la vincula conceptualmente con el jardín, refiriéndose al paso del tiempo y de las estaciones expresado por los cambios de color y textura de la vegetación.

Photos © M. Detiffe

The original house offered tiny openings to the garden. The back rooms, kitchen, bathroom, previously considered as utilitarian rooms, blocked the views of the garden.

La maison d'origine offrait des ouvertures minuscules sur le jardin. Les pièces du fond, la cuisine, la salle d'eau, considérées auparavant comme purement utilitaires, obstruaient la vue sur le jardin.

Das ursprüngliche Haus hatte winzige Öffnungen zum Garten. Die hinteren Zimmer, die Küche und das Badezimmer, die zuvor als Nutzräume angesehen wurden, blockierten die Aussicht auf den Garten.

La casa original tenía pequeñas aberturas al jardín. Las habitaciones traseras, cocina y baño, anteriormente consideradas exclusivamente funcionales, tapaban las vistas al mismo.

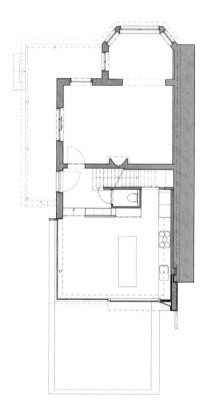

Ground floor plan

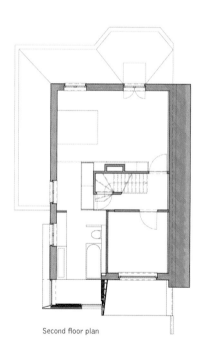

Second floor plan

Extension elevations

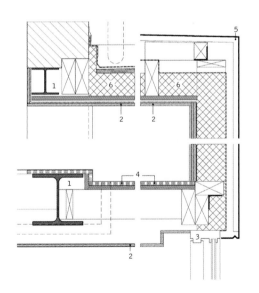

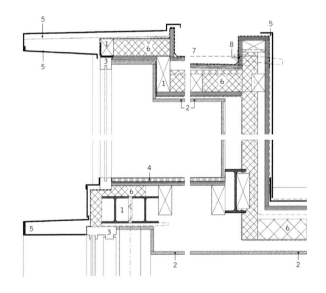

Section details

1. Steel structure
2. Plasterboard
3. Aluminium window frame
4. Tails

5. Corten
6. Insulation
7. Waterproof membrane
8. Rainwater evacuation

The design of the openings is enhanced by the selection of materials. Glazed sliding walls open the ground floor to the garden, whilst large windows on the first floor offer views of the outdoors.

Das Design der Öffnungen wird durch die Auswahl der Materialien unterstrichen. Schiebewände aus Glas öffnen das Erdgeschoss zum Garten und die großen Fenster im Obergeschoss bieten Ausblicke auf den Außenbereich.

Le design des ouvertures est mis en valeur par la sélection de matériaux utilisés. Des coulissants vitrés ouvrent le rez-de-chaussée sur le jardin, tandis que de grandes fenêtres offrent du premier étage des vues sur les extérieurs.

El diseño de las aperturas se realza con la selección de los materiales. Puertas correderas acristaladas abren la planta baja al jardín, mientras que los ventanales del primer piso tienen vistas al exterior.

The kitchen and the bathroom have been transformed into bright, inviting spaces. The kitchen is opened to the dining area and to the garden, whilst the bathroom faces the trees.

Die Küche und das Badezimmer wurden in helle, einladende Räume umgewandelt. Die Küche ist zum Essbereich und zum Garten geöffnet und das Badezimmer bietet Blick auf die Bäume.

La cuisine et la salle d'eau ont été transformées en espaces clairs, accueillants. La cuisine est ouverte sur la salle-à-manger et le jardin, tandis que la salle d'eau donne sur les arbres.

La cocina y el baño se han transformado en espacios acogedores y luminosos. La cocina se abre al comedor y al jardín, mientras que el baño tiene vistas a los árboles.

THE MEDIC'S HOUSE
A hidden gem nestled in the ordinary

LONDON, UNITED KINGDOM

TOTAL BUILDING AREA: 2260 sq ft – 210 m^2
EXTENSION AREA: 590 sq ft – 55 m^2 // 26% of total area

A growing family's need for additional space meant that their 1950's three-bedroom house had to be extended. The brief called for a large open-plan family space with light, views and access to a garden, as well as two additional bedrooms on the upper floor. The result is a large charcoal grey box at ground level with a full height glazed opening elevation facing the garden. A timber-clad sleeping pod at the first floor level is interlocked with the new volume below.

Suite aux besoins d'espace supplémentaire de la famille qui s'agrandissait, il fallait ajouter une extension à cette maison quatre pièces des années 1950. Il s'agissait de créer un grand espace familial ouvert qui permet d'avoir de la lumière, des vues et un accès au jardin, ainsi que deux chambres supplémentaires à l'étage. Il en résulte une grande « boîte » gris anthracite au niveau du sol comportant une élévation vitrée sur toute la hauteur face au jardin. Au niveau du premier étage, un module bardé de bois est imbriqué au nouveau volume en contrebas pour du couchage supplémentaire.

Das Bedürfnis einer wachsenden Familie nach mehr Platz führte zur Erweiterung ihres Hauses, das aus den 1950er-Jahren stammte und drei Schlafzimmer umfasste. Es sollten ein großer offener Familienraum mit Licht, Aussicht und Zugang zum Garten sowie zwei weitere Schlafzimmer im Obergeschoss entstehen. Das Ergebnis ist ein anthrazitfarbiger kastenförmiger Anbau im Erdgeschoss mit einer raumhohen verglasten Vorderseite, die zum Garten geöffnet werden kann. Ein holzverkleideter Schlafraum im Obergeschoss ist mit dem neuen darunter liegenden Raum verbunden.

La necesidad de espacio adicional por parte de una familia que ha ido creciendo, daba lugar a que tuviera que ampliarse su casa de tres dormitorios de la década de los cincuenta. La idea sugería un gran espacio familiar y abierto con luz, vistas y acceso a un jardín así como dos dormitorios adicionales en la planta superior. El resultado es una gran caja gris de pizarra a nivel del suelo con una altura acristalada que se abre mirando al jardín. Una caja revestida de madera que alberga los dormitorios está conectada con el nuevo volumen de la planta baja.

The overall composition was influenced by the ancient Greek theory of the "Golden Section" in order to provide a well-balanced and proportioned rear elevation.

La composition générale du bâtiment a été influencée par la théorie grecque antique du « nombre d'or » pour faire en sorte que l'élévation arrière soit équilibrée et proportionnée.

Die Gesamtkomposition wurde von der altgriechischen Theorie des „Goldenen Schnitts" beeinflusst, um eine ausgewogene und gut aufgeteilte Rückansicht zu erzielen.

Para conseguir un alzado trasero proporcionado y equilibrado, se siguió la antigua teoría griega de la proporción áurea en la composición global del proyecto.

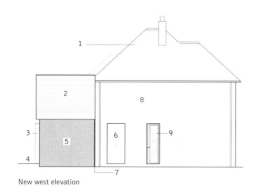

New west elevation

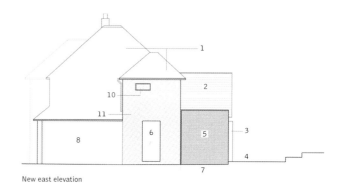

New east elevation

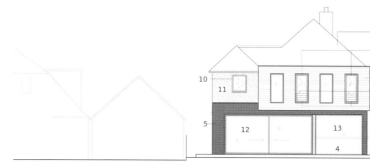

New north elevation

1. Existing roof retained and repaired as existing where necessary
2. Timber cladding
3. White fin
4. Tiled patio
5. Render in grey
6. Frameless glass
7. Shadow gap in dark grey
8. Existing brickwork retained
9. Metal frame glass door, powder coated in grey RAL7016
10. New metal window powder coated in grey
11. White render
12. Metal frame sliding glass doors, powder coated in grey RAL7016
13. Metal frame fixed glass pane, powder coated in grey RAL7016
14. Cables

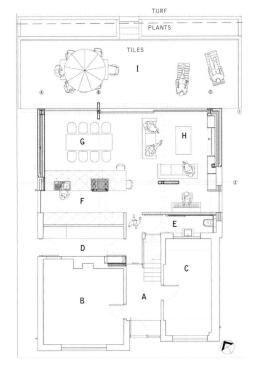

New ground floor plan

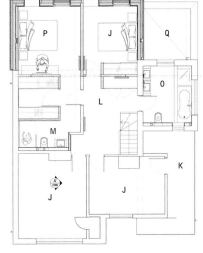

New first floor level

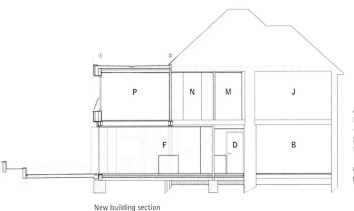

New building section

A. Entrance hall	J. Bedroom
B. Lounge	K. Eaves storage
C. Study	L. Landing
D. Utility room	M. En suite bathroom
E. Powder room	N. Walk-in-closet
F. Kitchen	O. Bathroom
G. Dining area	P. Master bedroom
H. Sitting area	Q. Roof
I. Patio	

The structure is hidden in strategically placed fins that suggest living zones within the open-plan space. Upstairs, the western red cedar addition allows for a lightweight structure that reduces the need for unsightly columns below.

Die Struktur ist in strategisch platzierten Mauervorsprüngen versteckt, die in dem offenen Raum Wohnbereiche andeuten. Im Obergeschoss ermöglicht das „Western Red Cedar"-Holz eine Leichtbauweise, wodurch keine unansehnlichen Säulen benötigt werden.

La structure est dissimulée dans des ailettes stratégiquement positionnées qui suggèrent des zones de vie au sein de l'espace ouvert. À l'étage, l'ajout en cèdre de l'Ouest permet une structure légère qui réduit le besoin de colonnes disgracieuses au-dessous.

La estructura se esconde en aleros verticales colocados estratégicamente sugiriendo que las zonas comunes conviven con el espacio abierto. En la primera planta, la extensión en madera de cedro canadiense permite una estructura ligera que reduce la necesidad de colocar antiestéticas columnas en la planta baja.

The flush threshold and continuous floor surface enhance the connection between the interior and the exterior. Large opaque glass panels to the sides allow filtered light to enter deep into the space.

Die ebenen Übergänge und die kontinuierliche Bodenfläche verstärken die Verbindung zwischen Innen- und Außenbereich. An den Seiten ermöglichen große Milchglasflächen den Eintritt von gefiltertem Licht, das tief in den Raum hineinfällt.

Le seuil affleurant et la surface continue au sol accentuent la connexion entre l'intérieur et l'extérieur. Sur les côtés, de grands panneaux vitrés opaques laissent entrer une lumière filtrée jusqu'au cœur de cet espace.

Se refuerza la conexión entre el interior y el exterior con un suelo continuo y sin desniveles. Los grandes paneles de cristal opaco a los lados permiten que la luz filtrada pueda entrar profundamente en el espacio.

ROMSEY ROAD

Art Deco meets a contemporary twist

192

LONDON, UNITED KINGDOM

TOTAL BUILDING AREA: 2900 sq ft – 270 m^2
EXTENSION AREA: 1655 sq ft – 154 m^2 // 57% of total area

An extension to a home built in the 1950's features a "simple but radical look". The brief was to bring into a tight and complicated layout of a family home a sense of space and calm. The renovated living spaces maximize the garden views. The design includes the use of the same floor material with flush thresholds and white finishes throughout to highlight spatial continuity, and allow a natural flow between the interior and the exterior. The ambiguity of interior and exterior spaces creates vitality in the tradition of modernist buildings like the Mies van der Rohe's Barcelona Pavilion.

Cette extension apportée à une maison construite dans les années 1950 a un aspect « simple mais radical ». Il s'agissait d'apporter une impression d'espace et de quiétude à la configuration compacte et complexe d'une maison familiale. Les espaces rénovés optimisent les points de vue sur le jardin. Dans le design, on trouve l'utilisation du même matériau pour les sols, avec des seuils affleurant et l'usage du blanc pour accentuer la continuité spatiale et permettre une fluidité naturelle entre l'intérieur et l'extérieur. L'ambiguïté des espaces intérieur et extérieur crée de la vitalité dans la tradition des constructions modernistes telles que le Pavillon de Barcelone de Mies van der Rohe.

Ein Anbau an ein Gebäude aus dem Jahr 1950 hat ein „schlichtes, aber radikales Aussehen". Einem engen und komplizierten Grundriss sollte ein Gefühl von Raum und Ruhe verliehen werden. Die renovierten Wohnbereiche bieten bestmögliche Ausblicke auf den Garten. Das Design umfasst die Verwendung des gleichen Bodenmaterials mit bündigen Übergängen sowie durchweg weiße Oberflächen, was die räumliche Kontinuität betont und einen fließenden Übergang zwischen Innen- und Außenbereichen entstehen lässt. Die Ambiguität von Innen- und Außenbereichen schafft eine Lebendigkeit in der Tradition moderner Gebäude, wie dem Barcelona-Pavillon von Mies van der Rohe.

La ampliación de una casa construida en la década de los cincuenta muestra un "aspecto sencillo pero radical". La idea era dar una sensación de espacio y tranquilidad al diseño estrecho y complicado de una vivienda familiar. Los espacios comunes remodelados maximizan las vistas al jardín. El diseño pasa por usar el mismo material del suelo con umbrales rasantes y acabados en blanco para resaltar la continuidad espacial y permitir el flujo natural entre el interior y el exterior. La ambigüedad de los espacios interiores y exteriores crea vitalidad en la tradición de los edificios modernistas como es el Pabellón de Barcelona de Mies van der Rohe.

The house was upgraded with new windows, doors and paint, and a limited colour and finishes palette of white and grey render and tiles to bring light and a sense of space into the house.

La maison a été modernisée par le biais du changement des fenêtres, des portes et des peintures. Une palette limitée de couleurs et de finitions avec des enduits et des carrelages blancs et gris contribue à apporter de la lumière et un sentiment d'espace à la maison.

Das Haus wurde mit neuen Fenstern, Türen und einem neuen Anstrich modernisiert, wobei die Farben und Oberflächen sich auf Putz und Fliesen in den Farben Weiß und Grau beschränken, um das Haus mit Licht zu füllen und ihm ein Gefühl von Raum zu verleihen.

La casa se ha renovado con nuevas ventanas, puertas y pintura, y una paleta limitada de acabados y color en blanco y gris además de azulejos, para atraer la luz y dar una sensación de espacio.

New ground floor plan

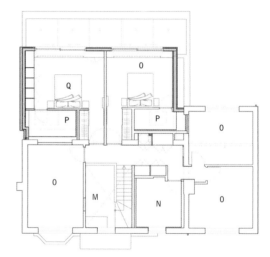

New first floor plan

A. Entrance
B. Storage
C. Study
D. Powder room
E. Garage
F. Side entrance
G. Utility room
H. Kitchen
I. Dining area
J. Sitting area
K. Lounge
L. Tiled terrace
M. Void
N. Family bathroom
O. Bedroom
P. En suite bathroom
Q. Master bedroom

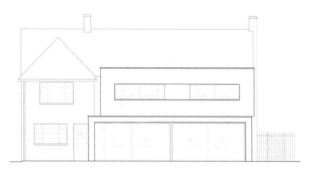

New south elevation

On the first floor, the extension stacks on top of the living spaces as a grey box containing two master bedrooms with en suite bathrooms. The extension also liberates space to create a new double height entrance and a staircase.

Der Anbau in der ersten Etage befindet sich in Form eines grauen Kastenbaus über den Wohnräumen und beherbergt zwei Master-Schlafzimmer mit dazugehörigen Badezimmern. Der Anbau schuf außerdem Platz für einen Eingangsbereich mit doppelter Raumhöhe und eine Treppe.

Au premier étage, l'extension est empilée sur les pièces de vie comme une « boîte » grise contenant les deux suites parentales et leur salle d'eau attenante. Elle libère également de l'espace pour la création d'une nouvelle entrée en double hauteur et d'un escalier.

En la primera planta, y sobre los espacios comunes, la extensión se asienta como una caja gris que alberga dos dormitorios principales con baños en suites. La ampliación también libera espacio para crear una nueva entrada a doble altura y una escalera.

On the ground floor the area of the kitchen and dining area is doubled, creating an expansive open living space. This area further extends onto a glass-covered patio and to the garden beyond.

Im Erdgeschoss wurde die Größe der Küche und des Essbereichs verdoppelt, wodurch ein weitläufiger offener Wohnbereich entstand. Dieser Bereich erstreckt sich bis auf eine mit Glas überdachte Terrasse und zu dem dahinter liegenden Garten.

Au rez-de-chaussée la surface de la cuisine et du coin repas est doublée, ce qui crée une pièce à vivre spacieuse et ouverte. Cette zone s'étend encore jusqu'à un patio vitré et, plus loin, jusqu'au jardin.

En la planta baja la zona de la cocina y el comedor se duplica, creando un espacio común amplio y abierto. Esta zona se extiende hacia un patio cubierto de cristal y hacia el jardín.

FOREST VIEW

A complete transformation has created a stunning residence unique in architecture and interior design

LONDON, UNITED KINGDOM

TOTAL BUILDING AREA: 4019 sq ft – 373 m²
EXTENSION AREA: 1037 sq ft – 96 m² // 26% of total area

The property boasts a striking rear extension with a ground floor "garden room" and two new bedroom suites, inclusive of the enlarged master bedroom. The deep, cantilevered eaves give the house a dramatic impression and offers protection against the elements. The rear gabled extensions are duplicated to achieve a balanced symmetry, whilst the wrap-around glazing ensures that the new downstairs room merges aesthetically with the garden.

Cette propriété bénéficie d'une extension arrière comprenant une Garden Room, pièce entre maison et jardin, au rez-de-chaussée, et deux nouvelles chambres, dont la suite parentale agrandie. Les larges corniches en porte-à-faux confèrent à la maison un air spectaculaire et offrent une protection contre les éléments. Les deux extensions à pignons à l'arrière sont identiques pour parvenir à une symétrie équilibrée, tandis que le vitrage panoramique permet à la nouvelle pièce du bas de se mêler esthétiquement au jardin.

Das Gebäude ist an der Rückseite mit einem markanten Anbau versehen. Dieser beherbergt ein „Gartenzimmer" im Erdgeschoss und zwei neue Schlafzimmer, darunter das vergrößerte Master-Schlafzimmer. Der tiefe, ausladende Dachvorsprung verleiht dem Haus einen dramatischen Eindruck und bietet Wetterschutz. Die Anbauten mit Giebeldach spiegeln sich, um eine ausgewogene Symmetrie zu erzielen, während die Rundumverglasung sicherstellt, dass das neue untere Stockwerk fließend in den Garten übergeht.

La propiedad disfruta de una notable ampliación en la parte de atrás con un "jardín de invierno" en la planta baja y dos nuevos dormitorios en suite, además de la ampliación del dormitorio principal. Los amplios aleros voladizos dan una impresión impactante de la casa y ofrecen protección contra los elementos. La ampliación trasera a dos aguas se duplica para conseguir una simetría equilibrada. El cierre acristalado permite que la nueva habitación de la planta baja se funda armoniosamente con el jardín.

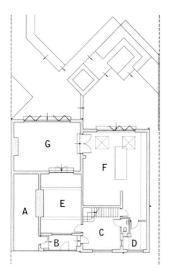

Original ground floor plan

Original first floor plan

Original second floor plan

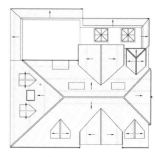

Original roof plan

A. Garage
B. Entrance
C. Entrance hall
D. Utility room
E. Lounge
F. Kitchen/dining
G. Family room
H. Master bathroom
I. Master bedroom
J. Bedroom
K. Bathroom

Original east elevation

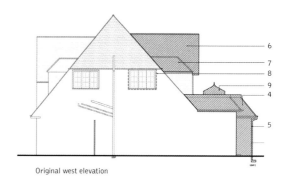

Original west elevation

Original south elevation

▨ Area to be removed
▨ Area to be blocked up
⬚ Window to be retained
⬚ Other features

1. Existing roof tiles carefully removed and stored. Upon strip out main contractor to confirm with structural engineer and architect existing rafters and roof build-up. Structural engineer to advise on sustainability and recommendations to tie in with the proposed new roof
2. Existing flank wall to be retained
3. Existing lanterns removed and carefully disposed of
4. Existing roof tiles, battens and rafters of lower roof to be removed
5. Existing RWP to be terminated and removed. Refer to proposed plans for new RWP positions and connections
6. Upon strip out main contractor to remove plasterboard ceiling and advise architect if insulation is between rafters or at ceiling joist level. Existing roof tiles are to be carefully removed and stored Upon strip out, main contractor to confirm with structural engineer and architect existing rafters and roof build up. Structural engineer to advise on suitability and recommendations to tie in with the proposed new roof

7. Roof to be carefully stripped around dormer and existing flank wall to be retained
8. Existing window to be retained and suitably protected during construction works
9. Existing lanterns to be removed and stored
10. Existing gable frontage removed
11. Existing dormers to be retained
12. Area of existing roof to be carefully stripped locally
13. Existing timber window to be removed and carefully protected and stored on site
14. Area to be infilled once doors have been removed. Infill bricks to match existing
15. Outline of new roof
16. Existing roof, fascia, and gutters to be removed
17. Existing rear wall to be carefully removed
18. Existing fascia, soffit and gutters to be removed
19. Existing door to be carefully removed and stored. Refer to proposed plans for setting out

200

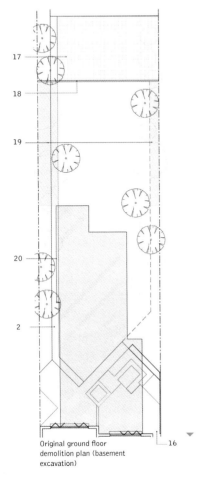

Original ground floor
demolition plan (basement
excavation)

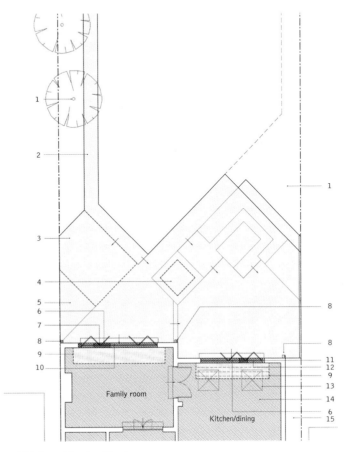

Original ground floor demolition plan

	Area to be removed
▓	Area to be blocked up
░	No access area
	Area to be protected
�.⌉	Other features

1. Upon excavation for basement all plants within affected area to be removed and preserved ahead of works. Task to be organized with client's landscape consultant

2. Upon excavation for the basement, carefully remove, protect and store affected paving slabs. Main contractor to reinstate paving area on completion of basement works, as landscaping plan (not shown). Main contractor to replace any damage slabs

3. Toy house approximately in this location to be carefully removed and stored in designated fenced storage area at the back of the site

4. Feature water ball to be carefully removed and stored in designated fenced storage area at the back of the site

5. Existing patio finish to be carefully removed and stored for client's use

6. Doors to be carefully removed and stored

7. Masonry infills. External facing brick to match existing and new openings to be made good

8. Existing RWP to be terminated and removed. Refer to proposed plans for new guttering and pipe work

9. Restricted zone. No personnel to advance beyond this zone. Dotted line indicates run of boarded protection to be erected by contractor

10. New window to be installed prior to construction of garden room. Following installation, window to be appropriately protected on the outer face during construction of garden room

11. Wall to be partially taken back once existing door is removed

12. Refer to proposed plans for new opening setting out

13. Existing lanterns to be removed and stored

14. When access is required for elements of the project within exiting kitchen and family room, main contractor to ensure appropriate protection is applied to the existing kitchen, flooring, television, doors, gas fires, etc. Protection methods to all be confirmed by architect prior continuing works

15. Leave existing slabs in place. To be removed at end of contract ready for new landscaping scheme

16. Restricted side access

17. Fenced storage area, exact location to be confirmed by architect

18. Temporary fence to be erected or the temporary relocation and protection of retained items during construction

19. Existing flowerbed and paving slabs in hatched area to be protected ahead of building works. Any damaged/affected area to be made good following completion works

20. Outline of proposed basement

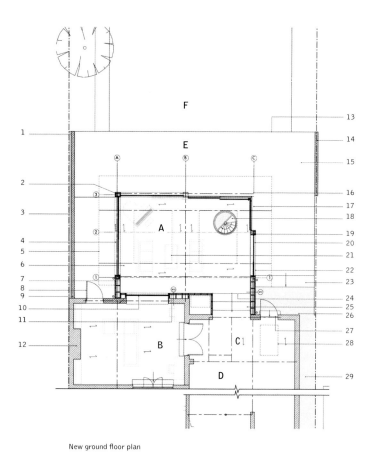

New ground floor plan

New first floor plan

Existing masonry walls
No access area
Skirting to match existing
Proposed masonry walls
Shadow gap detail

A. Garden room
B. Lounge
C. Kitchen
D. Dining area
E. Patio
F. Existing garden
G. Bathroom en suite
H. Dressing area
I. Bedroom
J. Family bathroom
K. Master bedroom
L. Storage

1. Proposed boundary wall to be 300 mm higher than the existing fence. Wall to be exposed brick on side to no.32, treatment on garden side to be confirmed
2. Structural pier to be boxed out in timber frame and clad in charred Siberian larch timber
3. 50 mm French drain between neighbour fence and proposed wall
4. Fineline "System 22" fixed glazing arranged as two equal panels
5. Outline of projected flat roof above
6. Internal and external floor to be flush in level. Finishes to be confirmed by interior/landscape designer and threshold details to be confirmed by architect via Fineline Aluminium
7. Recess omitted. Wall to be built out uniformly
8. Fineline "System 22" glazed door
9. Rainwater pipe and hopper omitted
10. Internal Fineline "System 22" fixed window. N.B window must be installed first sequentially
11. Existing external wall boxed out in timber frame
12. New fireplace to be provided by client
13. One or two steps down to existing garden. Detail to be confirmed by landscape designer
14. Treatment to extended wall to be confirmed

15. Internal/external flush level finishes in "Pocket Glamour" tile supplied by client. Landscape contractor to treat external finish with "Lithofin", supplied by Abbey Tiles
16. Size of Fineline door to be re-measured by Fineline Aluminium. 100 mm build out into consideration
17. Fineline sliding door "System 22"
18. 1500 mm diameter glass access door down to cellar. Glass access door to align with roof light above as indicated.
19. Timber frame wall encasing structural post. Wall to be finished with charred Siberian larch timber cladding
20. Fineline "System 22" fixed glazing
21. Structural opening required for 2400 (W) by 3000 (L) roof lights above
22. 400 mm high timber frame wall, built out 100 mm internally to be clad in charred Siberian larch timber
23. Steps to align with roof overhang above and glazing line
24. Extent of dropped ceiling
25. Three steps between garden room and kitchen. Bespoke joinery item by specialist contractor.
26. Rainwater pipe and hopper omitted
27. Fineline glazed access door

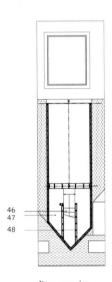

New mezzanine
storage level plan

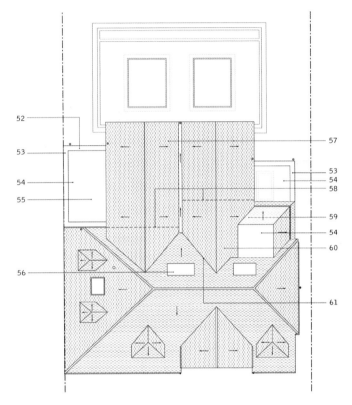

New roof plan

28. Outline of roof light above to achieve a min. U-Value 1.4w/M2k. supplied and fitted by Fineline. Main contractor to provide structural opening
29. Level entrance to rear of property
30. InstaGrufe green roof system. Main contractor to build up to and include water proof membrane
31. New roof light to achieve a U-Value of 1.4w/M2k
32. Stone strip detail
33. Sliding doors supplied and installed by Fineline to achieve a Min U-Value of 1.4w/M2k
34. Feature wall. Details to be confirmed. Main contractor to await confirmation of wall build up before construction
35. Fitted wardrobes to be supplied and installed by Small Bone of Devizes
36. Main contractor to remove existing ceiling lights and install new light fittings. Main contractor to also implement all associated electrical works in line with proposed lighting layout.
37. Main contractor to redecorate and make good as required to existing section of master bedroom
38. Lining to roof lights to be polyester powder coated in RAL8019

39. Main contractor to form double step to the lower level in bedroom. Nosing to be formed y others
40. RWP to run from first floor gable roof down to ground floor via hopper, picking up drainage from parapet wall
41. New roof light supplied and installed by Fineline to achieve a min. U-Value 1.4w/M2k. Main contractor to form curb and structural opening
42. Main contractor to confirm existing external wall build up upon strip out. New wall to be of same construction and tie in accordingly
43. Existing windows to be reinstated in different position
44. Bespoke wardrobe units by others
45. Main contractor to liaise with architect prior to setting out wall.
46. Staircase by others
47. M&E unit to be located in this zone
48. Short partition walls. Height to be determined
49. Existing window to be protected by plywood
50. Existing doors to be reinstated
51. Main contractor to ply off areas identified on strip out drawings to ensure construction workers only access specific zones/areas

52. Existing pitch roof stripped back, rafters removed and new parapet to be constructed above existing external wall. Brick to match existing
53. Stone coping
54. Sarnafil roof covering in lead grey 9500
55. Roof light omitted along with any associated structural elements
56. Existing dormer to be repositioned, centred on central valley of gables. Existing roof covering to be reused
57. Extent of new roof
58. Extent of existing roof
59. Roof to existing dormer raised and extended across to abut with new pitched roof
60. Existing tiles to be reinstated. If short fall, reclaimed tiles to match existing are to be used
61. Existing roof
Making good will be required to all areas that have been affected by construction work, in particular those junctions whereby existing roof meets new roof

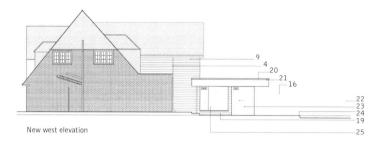

New west elevation

New south elevation

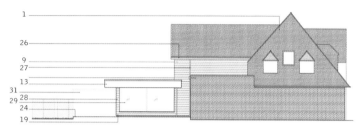

New east elevation

New section D-D

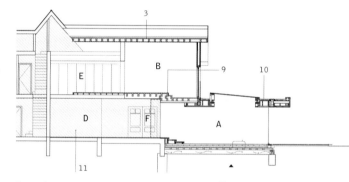

Proposed section B-B   ▨ Existing walls

1. Existing roof
   Making good will be required to all areas that have been affected by construction work, in particular those junctions whereby existing roof meets new roof
2. Line of roof pitch of existing dormer
3. Relocated existing window. All tiling/flashing details to be restored and all surrounding areas made good
4. Box profile RWP to be extended from hopper, polyester powder coated. RAL black 9005
5. Stone coping
6. Existing wall to be extended. Finish to be confirmed by landscape consultant
7. Structural pier to be boxed out in timber frame and clad in charred Siberian larch timber
8. Head of Fineline glazed access doors to align with underside of extended soffit of garden room
9. Charred Siberian larch timber
10. Sliding opening doors supplied and installed by Fineline to achieve a min. U-Value of 1.4w/M2k. Main contractor to ensure that head of glazing is lined below central valley of roof
11. Box profile RWP to be extended from hopper, polyester powder coated RAL black 9005
12. Glass balustrade arranged as a single plane of glazing, supplied and installed by Fineline.
13. New parapet wall formed in line with existing external wall
14. Fineline two-track sliding door "System 22"
15. Fineline "System 22" fixed glazing arranged as two equal panels

16. Proposed wall with exposed brick face on neighbour-facing side. Height to be increased 225 mm. Wall cladding to garden side to be confirmed by landscape designer
17. Existing fence
18. Head of Fineline glazed access doors to align with underside of steel
19. 400 mm high wall below fixed windows to be clad in charred Siberian larch timber. 100 mm plinth detail to be maintained constantly around dwarf wall and posts. Main contractor to take this build up into account when boxing in posts
20. InstaGrufe green roof system. Main contractor to build up to and including water prof membrane
21. Projected flat roof
22. Existing fence to boundary in distance to be retained and protected and during construction
23. Fineline one-track sliding door "System 22"
24. One or two steps down to garden level to be confirmed by landscape designer. Extract vents from under slab ventilation pipes to be accommodated into step
25. Fineline "System 22" fixed glazing arranged as two panels. Frame of larger panel to sit in line with frame of sliding panel when open
26. Black timber fascia
27. Box profile RWP's, hopper, polyester powder coated. Colour to be confirmed
28. Existing rendered wall extended. Wall treatment to be confirmed
29. Pier to be clad with charred Siberian larch timber

A. Garden room
B. Bedroom
C. Master bedroom
D. Dining area
E. Dressing room
F. Kitchen

1. Exposed Glulam ridge beam. Treated accordingly. Finish to be confirmed
2. Bespoke joinery item
3. First floor roof specification:
   - Roof tile to match existing roof
   - 25 x 50 mm batten
   - Roof breather membrane
   - 25 x 50 mm counter batten
   - 200 x 50 mm rafters (50 mm ventilation zone to be maintained)
   - Celotex 150 mm XR 4000 insulation between rafters
   - Vapour barrier
   - 12.5 TB 4000 Celotex
   - 15 mm Soundblock
4. Feature wall separating the dressing area and the master bedroom. Finish to be confirmed
5. Projecting wall. Finish to be confirmed

6. Wall to be extended 225 mm (3 bricks)
7. Feature recess within external timber frame wall to be omitted
8. Internal Fineline "System 22" fixed window. N.B. window must be installed prior to construction of garden room and suitably protected on recommencement of construction
9. Double step to lower balcony level. Detail to be confirmed
10. Garden room roof specification:
    - Grufe green roof module
    - Waterproof roofing membrane
    - 18 mm marine plywood
    - Timber firings laid to falls
    - 50 mm air layer to be maintained
    - Vapour control layer
    - 200 x 50 mm rafters to sit within web of structural steel
    - 175 mm Styrofoam LBH between joists
    - 25 mm timber battens
    - 15 mm Spacetherm
    - 9.5 Spacetherm plasterboard
    - Skim finish
11. Area not within works

The deep roof eaves of the ground floor extension have recessed lighting that enhances the form of the structure and creates a floating effect above the mostly glazed enclosure.

Der tiefe Dachvorsprung des Erdgeschossanbaus ist mit einer eingebauten Beleuchtung versehen, die Form des Baus betont und einen Schwebeeffekt über dem größtenteils verglasten Gebäude entstehen lässt.

Les débords de toiture en avancée de l'extension du rez-de-chaussée sont dotés d'un éclairage encastré qui fait ressortir la forme de la structure et crée un effet de flottaison au-dessus de l'enceinte majoritairement vitrée.

Los pronunciados aleros del tejado de la ampliación de la planta baja tienen luces empotradas que refuerzan la forma de la estructura y crean un efecto flotante sobre el cierre casi completamente acristalado.

The green sedum roof of the ground floor extension provides additional insulation and gives an attractive view from the new bedrooms on the first floor, whilst the skylights reinforce the open character of the garden room.

Das begrünte Dach des Erdgeschossanbaus bietet zusätzliche Isolierung und sorgt für einen angenehmen Ausblick aus den neuen Schlafzimmern der ersten Etage. Die Oberlichter verstärken den offenen Charakter des Gartenzimmers.

La toiture végétalisée, recouverte de sedum, de l'extension du rez-de-chaussée procure une isolation supplémentaire et offre une vue agréable depuis les nouvelles chambres du premier étage, tandis que les fenêtres de toit renforcent le caractère ouvert de la pièce du dessous.

El tejado ecológico de la extensión de la planta baja proporciona un aislamiento extra y da una vista atractiva desde los nuevos dormitorios del primer piso. Al mismo tiempo los tragaluces refuerzan el carácter abierto del jardín de invierno.

A first class finish is ensured throughout the new interior, incorporating the latest technology and imaginative design, which includes bespoke lighting and a sunken wine cellar, created flush with the tiled floor.

Der gesamte neue Innenbereich verfügt über eine hochwertige Ausstattung, die die neueste Technologie und fantasievolles Design in sich vereint. Dazu gehört die bereits erwähnte Beleuchtung und ein in den Boden eingelassener Weinkeller, der bündig mit dem Fliesenboden abschließt.

Une finition haut-de-gamme est assurée dans tout le nouvel intérieur, avec l'incorporation de technologies et de design imaginatifs de pointe, dont un éclairage sur-mesure et une cave-à-vins encastrée, à fleur du sol carrelé.

En el interior destacan los acabados de gran calidad, que incorporan tecnología punta y un diseño imaginativo, como la iluminación hecha a medida y la bodega excavada, a ras del pavimento cerámico del suelo.

ORAMA RESIDENCE

The transformation of a gracious victorian villa

SYDNEY, NEW SOUTH WALES, AUSTRALIA

TOTAL BUILDING AREA: 4349 sq ft – 404 m²
EXTENSION AREA: 1755 sq ft – 163 m² // 40.5% of total area

The extension of this Victorian villa responds to the changed needs of a family. Built in two stages, the project addresses the original villa as a distinct entity, enhancing its trim, white, and tailored design. By contrast, the new addition is minimal in form and detail with exposed concrete walls extending out into the garden. Separated by a century and a half, the two sections of the Orama residence stand as beautiful expositions of the best construction standards of their day.

L'extension de cette villa victorienne répond aux nouveaux besoins de là famille. Construit en deux temps, ce projet aborde la villa d'origine en tant qu'entité distincte, en faisant ressortir le côté ajusté, immaculé, sur-mesure de sa conception. Par contre, la nouvelle annexe est minimaliste au niveau de sa forme et de ses détails, avec ses murs en béton brut qui s'étendent vers le jardin. À un siècle et demi d'écart, les deux sections de la résidence Orama sont de belles représentations des meilleurs standards du bâtiment de leurs époques respectives.

Der Anbau dieser viktorianischen Villa erfüllt die neuen Bedürfnisse einer Familie. Das Projekt, das in zwei Phasen erbaut wurde, sieht die ursprüngliche Villa als selbstständige Einheit an und betont ihr schnörkelloses, weißes und individuelles Design. Im Gegensatz dazu sind Form und Details des neuen Anbaus mit Sichtbetonwänden, die sich bis in den Garten erstrecken, minimalistisch. Die beiden Bereiche der Orama-Residenz, die eineinhalb Jahrhundert voneinander trennen, sind wunderschöne Beispiele für die besten Baustandards ihrer Zeit.

La extensión de esta villa victoriana responde a las necesidades en constante cambio de una familia. Construido en dos fases, el proyecto aborda la villa original como una entidad distinta, mejorando su blanco y esbelto diseño hecho a medida. Por el contrario, la nueva extensión reduce al mínimo la forma y el detalle con paredes de hormigón visto que se extienden hacia el jardín. Separadas por un siglo y medio, las dos secciones de la residencia Orama se presentan como hermosas exposiciones de los mejores estándares de construcción de su tiempo.

SMART DESIGN STUDIO

Photos © Sharrin Rees

The new wing was designed and built with the same intricacy, attention to detail, and superb craftsmanship as the original villa, applied to modern methods of construction.

Der neue Flügel wurde, unter Verwendung moderner Bauweisen, mit der gleichen Komplexität, Detailliebe und hervorragenden Handwerkskunst entworfen und erbaut wie die ursprüngliche Villa.

La nouvelle aile a été conçue et construite avec la même délicatesse, le même souci du détail, et le même savoir-faire que la villa originale, en utilisant des méthodes modernes de construction.

La nueva ala fue diseñada y construida con la misma complejidad, atención al detalle y la magnífica artesanía que en la villa original, aplicada a los métodos modernos de construcción.

New west elevation

New north elevation

New building sections

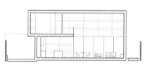

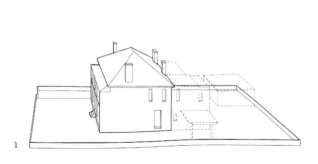

1

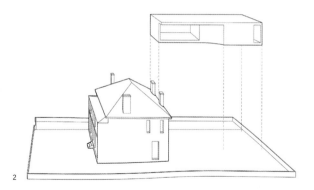

2

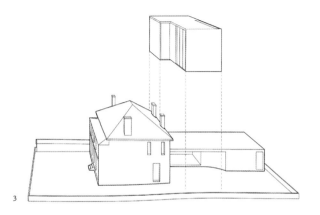

3

4

Design development diagrams

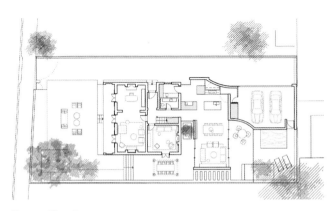

New ground floor plan

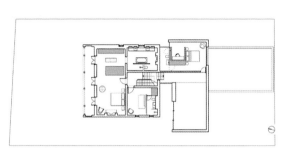

New first floor plan

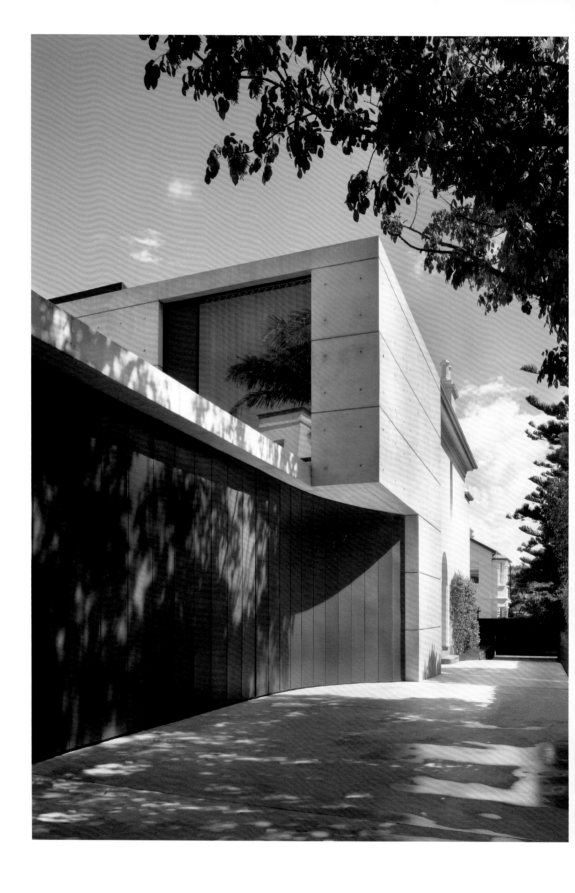

A striking double-height living area forms the nucleus of the extension, flowing into the garden. The bare concrete walls provide a dramatic backdrop for the client's incredible art collection.

Der Kern dieses Anbaus ist ein eindrucksvoller Wohnbereich mit doppelter Raumhöhe, der fließend in den Garten übergeht. Die Betonwände bieten eine dramatische Kulisse für die unglaubliche Kunstsammlung des Kunden.

Une remarquable pièce à vivre en double hauteur constitue le noyau de l'extension, qui se fond dans le jardin. Les murs en béton banché offrent une toile de fond spectaculaire pour l'incroyable collection d'œuvres d'art du client.

Una llamativa zona común de doble altura forma el núcleo de la extensión que desemboca en el jardín. Los muros de hormigón visto proporcionan un espectacular telón de fondo para la increíble colección de arte del cliente.

The material palette of concrete, glass, dark steel, and zinc beautifully complements the chic black and white scheme applied to the historic house.

Die Materialpalette aus Beton, Glas, dunklem Stahl und Zink fügt sich wunderbar in das elegante schwarz-weiße Farbschema des historischen Hauses ein.

La palette de matériaux comprenant le béton, le verre, l'acier de couleur sombre et le zinc vient compléter joliment l'élégant jeu de noir et blanc de la maison historique.

La paleta de materiales de hormigón, cristal, acero oscuro y zinc complementa perfectamente el elegante diseño en blanco y negro existente en la casa histórica.

Beautifully crafted elements of the historic house, such as the fireplaces, were retained. Other parts of the villa were updated with sensitively chosen fittings and fixtures to bring out the best of the old building.

Kunstvoll gefertigte Elemente des historischen Hauses, wie die Kamine, wurden erhalten. Andere Teile der Villa wurden mit sorgfältig ausgewählten Armaturen und Einbauten modernisiert, um das alte Gebäude voll zur Geltung zu bringen.

Des éléments de belle facture de la maison originale, tels que les anciennes cheminées, ont été conservés. D'autres parties ont été remises au goût du jour avec un équipement et des accessoires choisis avec soin pour mettre en relief les qualités de l'ancien bâtiment.

Se conservaron algunos maravillosos objetos de artesanía de la casa histórica tales como las chimeneas. Otras partes de la villa se han actualizado cuidadosamente con muebles y accesorios para respetar lo mejor del edificio antiguo.

S14 HOUSE

Transformation of a dilapidated house into an environmentally-friendly sensitive haven

SELANGOR, MALAYSIA

TOTAL BUILDING AREA: 4004 sq ft – 372 m²
EXTENSION AREA: 2336 sq ft – 217 m² // 58.5% of total area

A new two-storey addition to an existing structure sought to integrate a new home into an existing building, and establish a relationship with the trees around it, and the surrounding urban landscape. Not a single tree was removed before, during or after construction. This was in response to a design concept that was centred on working around the elements found on the site. Reinforced concrete and steel structures combine with existing and recycled materials available developing a rich architectural language that was meant to be an expression of the area's identity.

Une extension d'un étage ajoutée à une structure existante cherchait à intégrer une nouvelle famille dans un bâtiment existant, et à établir une relation avec les arbres et le paysage urbain environnants. Aucun arbre n'a été retiré avant, pendant ni après les travaux de construction, pour répondre au concept d'un design axé sur un travail qui prend en compte les éléments trouvés sur le site. Le béton armé et les structures en acier se combinent aux matériaux existants et recyclés disponibles, ce qui donne lieu à un langage architectural riche conçu pour être une expression de l'identité locale.

Ein neuer zweistöckiger Anbau an ein bestehendes Gebäude sollte ein neues Haus in ein bestehendes Haus integrieren und eine Verbindung zu den Bäumen, die sich um das Gebäude herum befinden, und die umliegende städtische Landschaft entstehen lassen. In keiner Bauphase wurde auch nur ein einziger Baum entfernt. Dies entsprach dem Designkonzept, das den Schwerpunkt darauf lag, um die auf dem Grundstück vorhandenen Elemente herumzubauen. Stahlbeton- und Stahlkonstruktionen entwickeln zusammen mit den verfügbaren bestehenden und recycleten Materialien eine edle Architektursprache, welche die Identität der Region ausdrücken soll.

El anexo de dos plantas busca integrarse con el edificio original formando un nuevo hogar. También establece una relación con los árboles que lo rodean y con el paisaje urbano colindante. Como respuesta a un concepto de diseño centrado en trabajar junto con los elementos que se encuentran en el terreno, se mantuvieron todos los árboles antes, durante y después de la construcción. Hormigón reforzado y estructuras de acero se combinan con materiales existentes y reciclados desarrollando un lenguaje arquitectónico muy rico que estaba destinado a ser una expresión de la identidad de la zona.

The site, located in a suburban area west of Kuala Lumpur had a dilapidated single-storey house on it. The extensive works to accommodate the new program and the limited budget made it critical that as much as possible of the original structure be reused.

Ce site, localisé dans une banlieue à l'Ouest de Kuala Lumpur, était occupé par une maison de plain-pied délabrée. De par le budget limité et les travaux considérables nécessaires pour répondre au nouveau programme, il était primordial de réutiliser autant d'éléments de la structure originelle que possible.

Auf dem in einem suburbanen Gebiet westlich von Kuala Lumpur gelegenen Grundstück befand sich ein baufälliges einstöckiges Haus. Die umfassenden Arbeiten zur Aufnahme des neuen Programms und das begrenzte Budget machten es erforderlich, so viel wie möglich vom ursprünglichen Bau wiederzuverwenden.

Originariamente en este emplazamiento a las afueras de Kuala Lumpur, en una zona suburbana al oeste de la ciudad, había una deteriorada casa de una sola planta. El presupuesto era limitado y el programa del proyecto implicaba grandes cambios. Para conseguir aunar ambos condicionantes, se reutilizó la antigua edificación lo máximo posible.

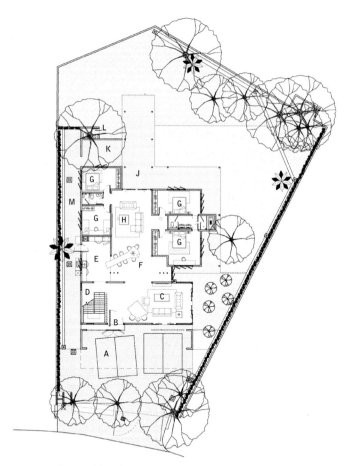

New ground floor plan

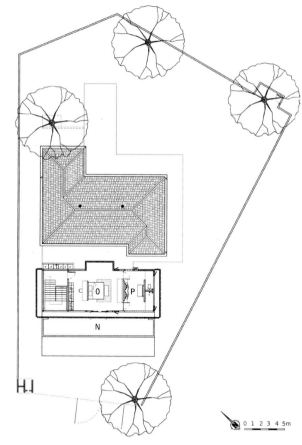

New first floor plan

A. Carport
B. Entrance
C. Formal living room
D. Staircase
E. Kitchen
F. Dining area
G. Bedroom
H. Family room
I. Bathroom
J. Veranda
K. Courtyard
L. Outdoor bathroom
M. Yard
N. Balcony
O. Master bedroom
P. Master bathroom

New front elevation

New side elevation

0 1 2 3 4 5m

The old and new buildings are seamlessly articulated in a succession of spaces that merge interior and exterior. The sense of space, the long sightlines enhance a fluid circulation between the different parts of the house.

Das alte und das neue Gebäude gehen in einer Abfolge von verbundenen Räumen, die Innen- und Außenbereiche miteinander verschmelzen lassen, nahtlos ineinander über. Das Raumgefühl und die langen Sichtachsen betonen einen fließenden Übergang zwischen den verschiedenen Teilen des Hauses.

L'ancien et le nouveau bâtiment s'articulent sans interruption dans une succession d'espaces qui unifient l'intérieur et l'extérieur. Le sentiment d'espace, les longues perspectives accentuent la circulation fluide reliant les différentes parties de la maison.

Ambos edificios, el antiguo y el contemporáneo, se articulan ininterrumpidamente en una sucesión de espacios donde se funde interior y exterior. La sensación de espacio y la inexistencia de barreras en el campo de visión realzan la fluida circulación entre las distintas partes de la vivienda.

The reuse of materials found on the site, the usage of vent blocks and formed concrete, as well as shading screens on the upper level are some of the elements that constitute the architectural language of the project.

Die Wiederverwendung von auf dem Grundstück vorgefundenen Materialien, die Nutzung von Lüftungsblocks und Formbeton sowie Sonnenschutzblenden im Obergeschoss sind einige der Elemente, welche die Architektursprache dieses Projekts auszeichnen.

La réutilisation de matériaux trouvés sur le site, l'usage de briques de ventilation et de béton banché, ainsi que de panneaux d'ombrage sur le niveau supérieur sont certains des éléments qui constituent le langage architectural de ce projet.

La reutilización de materiales encontrados en el terreno, el uso de respiraderos, hormigón encofrado y lamas para la protección solar en el piso superior, son algunos de los elementos que constituyen el lenguaje arquitectónico del proyecto.

FEISTEINVEIEN

Preserving the original house distinctive identity

STAVANGER, NORWAY

TOTAL BUILDING AREA: 1615 sq ft – 150 m^2
EXTENSION AREA: 1356 sq ft – 126 m^2 // 84% of total area

This extension to an existing single-family home was intended to make room for a growing family in a city, which has become increasingly dense over the last decades due to the economic boom related to the area's oil industry. The building authorities accepted an extension beyond the original restrictions, but wanted a modern expression. The concept of the project defines a modular extension that helps redefine the functional program of the house without obscuring the original character of the existing building. Rather, it lets it take centre stage as the heart of the home.

Le but de cette extension de maison unifamiliale était de prévoir de l'espace pour le développement d'une famille en milieu urbain, la ville s'étant densifiée progressivement depuis quelques décennies de par le boom économique lié à l'industrie pétrolière locale. Le concept de ce projet prévoit une extension modulaire qui aide à redéfinir le programme fonctionnel de la maison sans occulter le caractère original du bâtiment existant. Au contraire, elle lui permet d'occuper une place centrale au cœur de la maison.

Der Anbau an ein bestehendes Einfamilienhaus sollte mehr Platz für eine wachsende Familie schaffen. Die Familie lebt in einer Stadt, die in den letzten Jahren aufgrund des wirtschaftlichen Booms der Ölindustrie in der Region immer enger wurde. Die Baubehörde erlaubte einen Anbau, der über die ursprünglichen Beschränkungen hinausging, wünschte sich aber einen modernen Ausdruck. Das Projektkonzept definiert einen modularen Anbau, der das Funktionsprogramm des Hauses neu festlegt, ohne dabei den ursprünglichen Charakter des bestehenden Gebäudes zu verdecken. Stattdessen stellt das Konzept den ursprünglichen Bau als Herz des Familien-Wohnsitzes in den Mittelpunkt.

La bonanza económica relacionada con la industria del petróleo de la zona ha originado un aumento de la densidad de población en la ciudad en las últimas décadas. Por ello, el objetivo de esta ampliación de una vivienda unifamiliar urbana existente era dar cabida a una familia en crecimiento. Las autoridades urbanísticas aceptaron una extensión más allá de las restricciones originales, pero querían una construcción moderna. El concepto del proyecto define una extensión modular que ayuda a redefinir el programa funcional de la casa sin ocultar el carácter original del edificio existente. Más bien, permite que el espacio central sea el corazón de la vivienda.

Conceptual photomontage

The authorities and the architects agreed in that the existing building would be preserved intact to honour the architectural heritage of the area. Extension and addition stand out from each other by contrasting colours.

Die Baubehörde und die Architekten vereinbarten, dass das bestehende Gebäude intakt erhalten bleibt, um das architektonische Erbe der Region zu würdigen. Erweiterung und Anbau setzen sich durch kontrastierende Farben voneinander ab.

Les autorités locales et les architectes ont opté pour que le bâtiment d'origine soit préservé intact en hommage au patrimoine architectural de la région. L'extension et l'annexe se distinguent l'une de l'autre par leurs couleurs contrastées.

Las autoridades y los arquitectos estuvieron de acuerdo en preservar el edificio existente por respeto a la herencia arquitectónica de la zona. La extensión y los añadidos destacan uno del otro debido al contraste de colores.

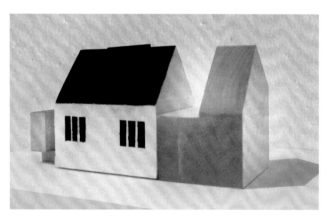

Conceptual scale model

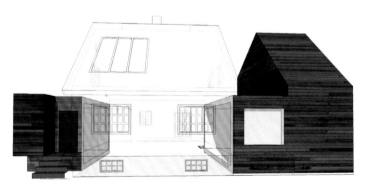

Conceptual rendering

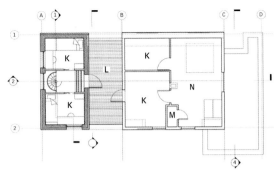

New first floor plan

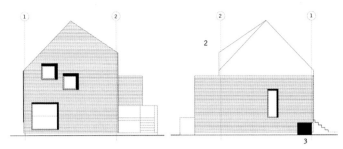

New north elevation   New south elevation

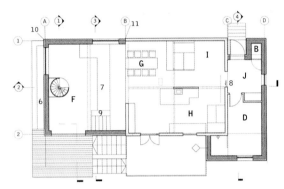

New ground floor plan

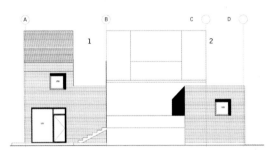

New east elevation

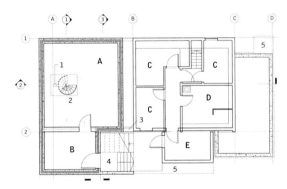

New basement floor plan

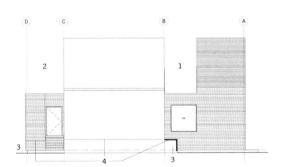

New west elevation

A. Basement room
B. Storage
C. Available space
D. Bathroom
E. Laundry room
F. Lounge
G. Dining area
H. Kitchen
I. Home office
J. Entry
K. Bedroom
L. Terrace
M. Toilet
N. Living area

1. Rough-sawn wood column
2. Foundation under spiral stair and column
3. Maintenance and ventilation hatch
4. Flooring with slope
5. Line of floor above
6. Skylight
7. Space between wall and stairs to accommodate modular sofa (Modern Living)
8. Frosted glass sliding door
9. Integrated TV screen
10. Wood boards to be aligned and mitred when turning corners.
11. Extension cladding starts 40 mm away from existing house cladding

1. Heights of ridge and cornice must be as those of existing house
2. All type V03 windows to be installed as deep into wall from exterior face as possible. All other windows to be installed as close to the exterior face of the wall as possible
3. Cantilever
4. Transition line between cladding and foundation in new construction to be aligned with transition line in existing building

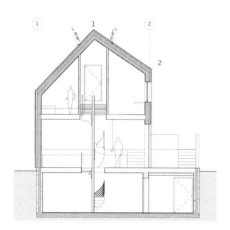

Section 1

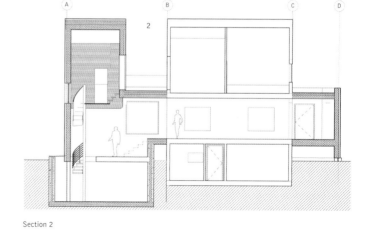

Section 2

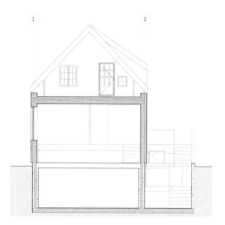

Section 3

1. Roof ventilation through wood boards
2. Heights of ridge and cornice must be as those of existing house
3. New floor at same level as existing

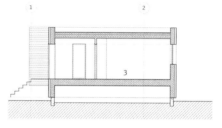

Section 4

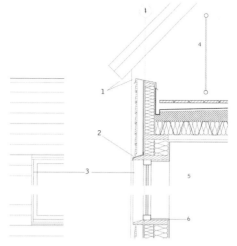

Wall section detail at roof terrace

1. It is important that the highest point of the extension building isn't higher than the lowest point of the existing building's eaves
2. Flashing to be finished in black as unnoticeable as possible
3. Surrounds of window openings (20 110 mm) to be finished to match building cladding
4. Guardrails fastened to building's walls
5. All windows to be set as deep into the walls as possible
6. 12 mm thick interior frame around windows to be painted white to match walls

The steel spiral staircase makes a strong design statement, while connecting all three levels of the addition through a minimal footprint.

Die Stahlwendeltreppe ist ein starkes Design-Statement und verbindet zugleich alle drei Ebenen des Ergänzungsbaus mit minimalem Fußabdruck.

L'escalier métallique en colimaçon constitue une affirmation conceptuelle forte, tout en reliant les trois niveaux de l'extension avec un encombrement minimum.

Destaca la fuerte presencia de la escalera de caracol de acero que une las tres plantas de la vivienda ocupando una superficie mínima.

The wood surfaces of the extension's interior are given a warm, light tint to achieve an inviting and homely atmosphere, whilst the steel spiral staircase and glass steps add a note of sophistication.

Die Holzoberflächen im Inneren des Anbaus verleihen ihm einen warmen, hellen Farbton, der eine einladende und gemütliche Atmosphäre entstehen lässt. Die Wendeltreppe aus Stahl und die Stufen aus Glas verleihen ihm ein elegantes Flair.

On a choisi des teintes chaudes et claires pour les surfaces en bois de l'intérieur de l'extension pour créer une ambiance accueillante et conviviale, l'escalier métallique en colimaçon et les marches en verre ajoutant une note de sophistication.

Para lograr un ambiente acogedor y hogareño, se aplicó un tinte claro y cálido a las superficies de madera del interior de la extensión. La nota de sofisticación la añade la escalera de caracol de acero con peldaños de cristal.

TWO HOMES IN ONE
With clarity

RENNES, FRANCE

TOTAL BUILDING AREA: 1722 sq ft −160 m²
EXTENSION AREA: 753 sq ft − 70 m² // 44% of total area

The project involving the construction of a new semi-detached house is located in a dense residential area formed by small businesses and single-family houses. The property, with an existing house dating from early 20th century, is set back from the street, generating a screen of vegetation that helps detach the house from the urban atmosphere. The new construction incorporates the lines of the existing building, including the slopes of the pitched roof and the design of the dormer window. The extension allows for the creation of a passageway on the ground floor and a glassed-in area on the first floor, where the existing house and the new construction meet.

Ce projet de construction d'une maison mitoyenne est situé dans une zone résidentielle dense composée de petites entreprises et de maisons unifamiliales. La propriété, dans laquelle la maison d'origine date du début du XXe siècle, est en retrait par rapport à la rue, ce qui génère un écran de végétation permettant de détacher la maison de l'atmosphère urbaine. La nouvelle construction incorpore les lignes générales du bâtiment existant, dont les pentes du toit à deux versants et le design de la mansarde. L'extension permet la création d'un passage au rez-de-chaussée et d'une zone fermée vitrée au premier étage, à la rencontre de la construction existante et de la nouvelle.

Das Projekt, das den Bau einer Doppelhaushälfte umfasste, ist in einer dicht bebauten Wohngegend vorzufinden, die sich aus kleinen Gewerbebetrieben und Einfamilienhäusern zusammensetzt. Das Grundstück mit einem bestehenden Haus aus dem frühen 20. Jahrhundert liegt zurückgesetzt von der Straße und wird durch die Vegetation von der urbanen Atmosphäre abgeschirmt. Der neue Bau nimmt die Linien des bestehenden Gebäudes auf, darunter die Schrägen des Giebeldachs und das Design der Mansardenfenster. Der Anbau bot die Möglichkeit, im Erdgeschoss einen Verbindungsgang und im Obergeschoss einen verglasten Bereich zu kreieren, in dem das bestehende Gebäude und der neue Bau aufeinandertreffen.

Ubicado en una densa zona residencial donde conviven pequeños negocios y casas unifamiliares, este proyecto consistía en la construcción de una nueva vivienda pareada. La finca, con una casa de principios del s. XX, está apartada de la calle, separada de la misma por vegetación, lo que ayuda a aislar la vivienda del ambiente urbano. La nueva construcción incorpora las líneas del edificio existente, incluyendo las curvas en el tejado y el diseño de la mansarda. La casa original y la nueva construcción se unen por un pasaje en la planta baja y una zona acristalada en la primera planta.

CLÉMENT BACLE ARCHITECTE

Photos © Martin Argyroglo

Urban planning regulations accepted an extension of the existing building to the property line. The architectural challenge is to provide a semi-detached dwelling, which only stands out for its contemporary language, but with no strong break.

Die städtebaulichen Vorgaben erlaubten eine Erweiterung des bestehenden Gebäudes bis zur Grundstücksgrenze. Die architektonische Herausforderung liegt darin, eine Doppelhaushälfte zu entwerfen, die sich durch ihre zeitgenössische Sprache auszeichnet, aber keinen starken Bruch darstellt.

Les règles de planification urbaine autorisaient une extension du bâtiment existant dans les limites de la propriété. Le défi architectural consiste à fournir une habitation mitoyenne qui ne se démarque que par son langage contemporain, sans rupture forte.

La regulación de la planificación urbanística aceptó la ampliación del edificio existente en el terreno de la propiedad. El desafío arquitectónico es conseguir una vivienda pareada que destaque exclusivamente por su lenguaje contemporáneo, sin romper con el diseño anterior.

Site plan

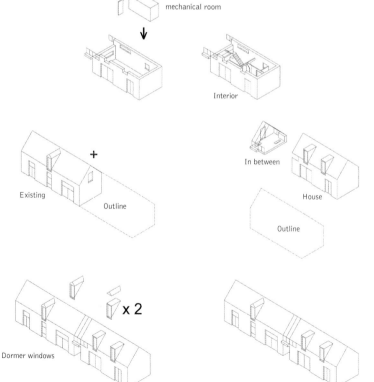

Bathroom – mechanical room

Interior

Existing

Outline

+

In between

House

Outline

Dormer windows

x 2

Diagrams

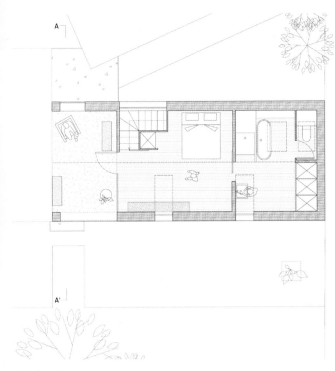

First floor plan

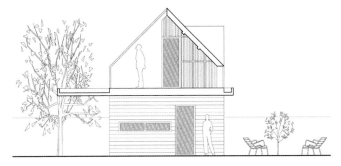

Section A-A

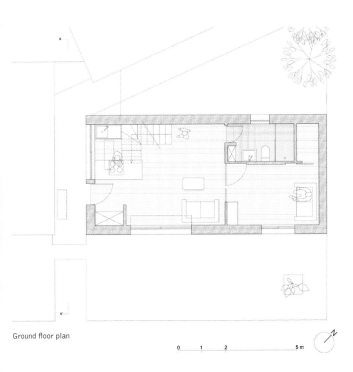

Ground floor plan

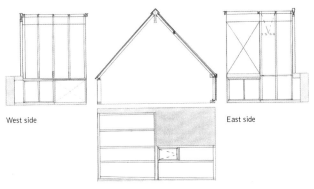

West side

East side

Glass roof details

0 1 2   5 m

The ground floor offers two bright rooms, which open onto the garden to the east. These two spaces, separated by a double door, form the daytime spaces. The kitchen is housed under the staircase on the south wall, which delimits the transitional space between the two homes.

Das Erdgeschoss umfasst zwei helle Zimmer, die sich zu dem im Osten liegenden Garten öffnen. Diese beiden Räume, die durch eine Doppeltür voneinander getrennt sind, sind die tagsüber genutzten Räume. Die Küche ist unter der Treppe an der südlichen Wand untergebracht, die den Übergangsbereich zwischen den beiden Häusern begrenzt.

Le rez-de-chaussée offre deux pièces qui ouvrent à l'Est sur le jardin. Ces deux espaces, séparés par une double porte, forment les espaces de jour. La cuisine est logée sous la cage d'escalier sur le mur Sud, qui délimite l'espace de transition entre les deux maisons.

La planta baja alberga dos luminosas estancias que se abren al jardín por el este. Estas dos salas, separadas por una puerta de dos hojas, forman la zona de día. La cocina se encuentra bajo la escalera en la pared sur, que delimita el espacio de transición entre los dos hogares.

On the first floor, a bedroom and a bathroom are nestled under the roof, each with a dormer, whilst a skylight, connecting the existing and new slate roofs brings abundant natural light into the interior.

Im Obergeschoss mit gemütlichen Dachschrägen liegen ein Schlafzimmer und ein Badezimmer, die jeweils über ein Mansardenfenster verfügen. Ein Oberlicht verbindet das bestehende Schieferdach mit dem alten und sorgt dafür, dass der Innenraum lichtdurchflutet ist.

Au premier étage, une chambre et une salle d'eau sont nichées sous le toit, bénéficiant d'une mansarde chacun, tandis qu'une fenêtre de toit, lien entre la toiture existante et la nouvelle, apporte une abondance de lumière naturelle à l'intérieur.

En el primer piso, un dormitorio y un baño están alojados bajo el tejado, cada uno en una buhardilla. Un tragaluz, que conecta los tejados de pizarra originales con los nuevos, aporta abundante luz natural al interior.

THE OLD FARMHOUSE
Family farmhouse breathes new life

FAICHEM, SCOTTISH HIGHLANDS

TOTAL BUILDING AREA: 3649 sq ft – 339 m²
EXTENSION AREA: 3025 sq ft – 281 m² // 83% of total area

A substantial renovation and extension of an original farmhouse building has been designed to embrace the stunning vistas of the Scottish Highlands. The original house is reinstated at the heart of a tripartite composition. It is flanked by two distinctive and contemporary larch-clad barn-like structures and two frameless glazed bridges between the buildings. These bridges form corridors of light and establish a conceptual and visual separation between old and new. Sharp detailing is in synthesis with subtle reference to the local vernacular; the scheme sits sensitively and harmoniously in the larger rural context without becoming a pastiche of the historical.

Une rénovation et extension importante sur un corps de ferme a été conçue pour profiter de vues sublimes sur les Highlands d'Écosse. La maison d'origine retrouve sa position au cœur d'une composition tripartite. Elle est flanquée de deux structures originales et contemporaines ressemblant à des granges bardées de mélèze et de deux ponts vitrés à cadres masqués qui les relient entre elles. Ces passerelles constituent des couloirs de lumière et établissent une séparation conceptuelle et visuelle entre l'ancien et le nouveau. Un souci du détail se mêle à de subtiles références au style local ; ce programme s'inclut délicatement et harmonieusement dans le contexte rural général sans jamais verser dans un pastiche de l'historique.

Die umfassende Renovierung und Erweiterung eines ursprünglichen Bauernhauses sollte die fantastischen Ausblicke auf die schottischen Highlands zur Geltung bringen. Das ursprüngliche Haus findet sich im Herzen einer dreiteiligen Komposition wieder. Es wird von zwei markanten und zeitgenössischen Gebäuden im Scheunenstil mit Lärchenholzverkleidung und zwei rahmenlosen verglasten Brücken zwischen den Gebäuden flankiert. Die Brücken bilden Lichtkorridore und stellen eine konzeptuelle und visuelle Trennung von Alt und Neu dar. Die scharfen Linien sind eine dezente Bezugnahme auf den traditionellen Baustil der Region. Das Konzept fügt sich sensibel und harmonisch in den größeren ländlichen Kontext ein, ohne die Geschichte zu persiflieren.

Con el objetivo de maximizar las increíbles vistas de las Highlands escocesas se ha diseñado una remodelación considerable del edificio de una granja y una extensión del mismo. La casa original se ha reinstaurado en el centro de una composición tripartita. Está flanqueada por dos estructuras contemporáneas diferentes entre si, pero revestidas en madera de alerce y cuya forma recuerda a un granero. Los tres edificios se unen por puentes acristalados sin marcos. Estos puentes forman un pasillo de luz y establecen una separación visual y conceptual entre lo nuevo y lo antiguo. Los detalles marcados están en combinación con las sutiles referencias a la tradición local; el programa se asienta con tacto y armonía en el gran contexto rural sin llegar a ser un pastiche de lo histórico.

PAPER IGLOO ARCHITECTURE AND DESIGN

Photos © David Barbour

The family home is situated on the southern slopes of a glacial hillside. The lure of the site lies in the timeless panoramic mountain views to the south and west.

La maison familiale est située sur le versant Sud d'une colline glaciaire. L'attrait du site se trouve dans les vues panoramiques intemporelles des massifs au Sud et à l'Ouest.

Der Familien-Wohnsitz befindet sich an den Südhängen eines Gletschers. Der Reiz dieses Standorts liegt an der zeitlosen Panoramaaussicht auf die Berge in südlicher und westlicher Richtung.

La vivienda familiar se encuentra en la ladera sudeste de una colina glaciar. El atractivo del emplazamiento reside en sus atemporales vistas panorámicas a las montañas al sur y al oeste.

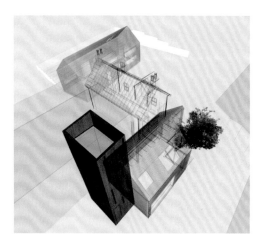

Computer generated rendering. Aerial view

Computer generated rendering. South view

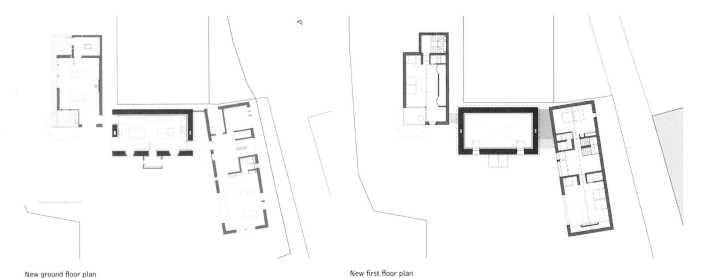

New ground floor plan

New first floor plan

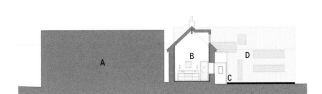

New section A

New south-east elevation

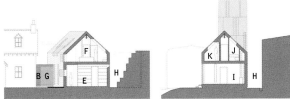

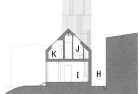

New section B

New section C

New south-west elevation

A. Timber barn one
B. Old farmhouse/
   kitchen-dining area
C. Porch
D. Timber barn two
E. Timber barn two/
   bedroom-day room
F. Timber barn two/bedroom

G. Glazed link
H. Path
I. Timber barn one/living room
J. Timber barn one/water closet
K. Timber barn one/shower
L. Corten circulation tower
M. Shed

0 1 2   5 m

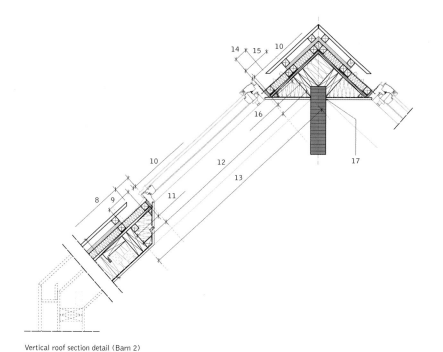

Vertical roof section detail (Barn 2)

Horizontal roof section detail (Barn 2)

1. 125 mm frame to batten above breather membrane
2. 30 mm between battens
3. 1180 between battens
4. Velux frame size = 1140
5. Structural opening as built = 1155
6. Only 15 mm wider than Velux frame size
7. 30 mm flashing to cladding
8. 125 mm frame to cladding
9. 190 mm between battens
10. 20 mm frame to batten
11. 213 overhang
12. Velux frame size = 1180
13. 1646 (466 mm more than Velux frame)
14. 100 mm frame to cladding
15. 210 mm frame to batten
16. 222 overhang
17. Plasterboard to start at exact position of adjacent plasterboard in plane of roof

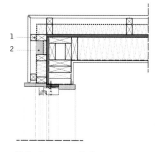

Timber barn one, gutter/ downpipe typical plan detail

1. Dash-dot line of gutter above in blue
2. Site assembled stainless steel downpipe
   - Joined to guttering by the client
   - Downpipes fixed back to 75 mm battens either side with prefabricated fixing plates
   - If possible add 25 mm thick insulation layer behind downpipe
   - Note: Tyvek to extend behind downpipe to retain continuous layer over building elevation

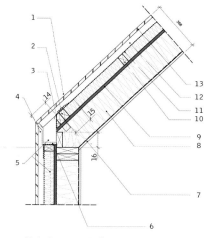

Timber barn one, gutter/ eaves typical section detail

1. Removable 500 mm wide section of cladding at max. 3 m intervals along elevation to allow access to gutter for maintenance/cleaning of debris
2. 2 No 75 x 45 mm battens trimmed to suit roof slope. 1 No untrimmed 75 x 45 mm batten to take eaves carrier
3. Tyvek eaves carrier nailed to horizontal batten and overhanging gutter with breather membrane overlapping by min. 150 mm
4. Note: vertical batten cut back to 30 mm thick at top to provide space for gutter
5. Site assembled stainless steel guttering and downpipes:
   - Guttering supplied pre-joined by the client
   - Downpipes in positions as shown on plumbing/drainage drawing, fixed back to 75 mm vertical battens either side
   - Note: Tyvek to extend behind downpipe to retain continuous layer over building elevation
6. Gutter intermittently supported on strips of 18 mm WBP running back to front at max. 400 centres
7. 12.5 mm foil backed plasterboard with skim, paint finish (plaster stop beads around all window openings/exposed corners)
8. 47 x 195 mm C16 rafters at 610 mm centres to engineer's specification and details with 47 x 195 mm bridle on flat at each end of Velux opening with Simpson strong tie angle brackets.
   195 mm kingspan insulation friction fitted between rafters and edges sealed with frame sealant as walls
9. 18 mm WBP plywood sheeting
10. 75 x 45 mm treated horizontal battens fixed through insulation back to main structural frame at max. 600 mm centres in both directions with min. 125 mm long fixings
11. Tyvek UV façade breather membrane or similar approved
12. 45 x 45 mm treated vertical battens fixed at max. 600 mm centres
13. 20 mm thick Siberian larch horizontal rain screen cladding with max. 5 mm gaps between boards
14. Approx. 145 mm overhang
15. 150 Tyvek overlap to eaves carrier
16. 110 to edge of rafter

Roof build up: Min. U-value 0.18W/M2K

The colour of autumn bracken, a Corten clad circulation and observatory tower abuts one barn; hard-edged, discreetly tapering walls allude to the previous light agricultural industry of the area now gone.

Eine Scheune zeichnet sich durch einen mit Cortenstahl verkleideten Aussichtsturm in der Farbe herbstlichen Farns aus. Die kantigen, sich dezent verjüngenden Wände spielen auf die frühere leichte Landwirtschaft in der Region an, die heute nicht mehr vorhanden ist.

De la couleur des fougères automnales, le campanile de communication et d'observation bardé d'acier Corten jouxte l'une des granges ; des murs aux arêtes verticales vives, discrètement effilés vers le haut, font référence à l'agriculture paysanne autrefois pratiquée dans la région et aujourd'hui disparue.

Del color del helecho en otoño, una torre observatorio revestida en acero corten delimita uno de los graneros; sus perfiles agudos y paredes discretamente estrechas evocan a la anterior industria agrícola del área, hoy desaparecida.

A considered, thoughtful internal layout and strategically placed skylights and windows ensure no space is without day lighting and garden views, whilst the two glazed bridges between the buildings form corridors of light, guiding the eye and occupant through the dwelling.

Eine durchdachte, ausgeklügelte räumliche Aufteilung im Innenbereich und strategisch platzierte Oberlichter und Fenster stellen sicher, dass jeder Raum mit Tageslicht und Aussicht auf den Garten versehen ist. Die beiden verglasten Brücken zwischen den Gebäuden bilden Lichtkorridore und führen das Auge und den Bewohner durch die Wohnstätte.

Grâce à une configuration réfléchie, attentionnée, et à des fenêtres de toit et ouvertures stratégiquement positionnées, aucun espace n'est privé de lumière du jour ni de vue sur le jardin, tandis que les deux ponts vitrés entre les bâtiments forment des couloirs de lumières, guidant le regard et l'occupant à travers la résidence.

Un diseño interno bien pensado y considerado, con ventanas y tragaluces estratégicamente situados, asegura que todos los espacios tienen luz natural y vistas al jardín. Los dos puentes de cristal entre los edificios forman pasillos de luz que atraen la mirada y conducen al ocupante a través de la vivienda.

FARMHOUSE AT MODOC SPRING
Adaptive reuse

ELVERSON, PENNSYLVANIA, UNITED STATES

TOTAL BUILDING AREA: 4929 sq ft – 458 m²
EXTENSION AREA: 1655 sq ft – 154 m² // 33.5% of total area

A sensitive renovation of an existing farmhouse in a rural seven-acre site surrounded by protected farmland was undertaken to accommodate home offices and bedrooms for children. The contemporary notions of family room and master suite were housed in a new two-storey addition. This addition acts as a threshold from a new entry to the site beyond, and along with the existing house and adjacent guest cottage, captures space around a new patio, creating protected and intimate outdoor space from which to enjoy idyllic landscape.

La rénovation respectueuse d'une ancienne ferme sur un site rural de près de trois hectares entouré d'une zone agricole protégée a été mise en œuvre pour accueillir des bureaux à domicile et des chambres pour enfants. Les notions contemporaines de chambre familiale et de suite parentale ont été intégrées dans une nouvelle annexe sur deux niveaux. Celle-ci fait office de seuil depuis un nouvel accès vers le site agricole et tout comme la maison d'origine et sa maison d'hôtes adjacente, capture l'espace dans l'enceinte d'un nouveau patio en créant un espace extérieur protégé et intime à l'abri duquel on peut profiter de la vue sur un paysage idyllique.

Ein bestehendes Landhaus auf einem ländlichen, sieben Morgen umfassenden Grundstück, das von geschützten Landwirtschaftsflächen umgeben ist, wurde sensibel renoviert, um Platz für Home Offices und Kinderzimmer zu schaffen. Die zeitgenössischen Konzepte eines Familienzimmers und eines Master-Schlafzimmers wurden in einem neuen zweistöckigen Anbau untergebracht. Dieser Anbau dient von einem neuen Eingang aus als Schwelle zum dahinter liegenden Teil des Gebäudes. Zusammen mit dem bestehenden Haus und dem daneben liegenden Gästehaus umschließt der Anbau eine neue Terrasse und bildet so einen geschützten und privaten Außenbereich, von dem aus man die idyllische Landschaft genießen kann.

En un terreno de cerca de tres hectáreas, rodeado de tierras de cultivo protegidas, se realizó una delicada restauración de una granja existente. El objetivo era dar cabida a zonas de trabajo y dormitorios para niños. La sala de estar y dormitorio principal, con su aire contemporáneo, se albergaron en la ampliación de dos pisos. Esta no solo actúa como el umbral de una nueva entrada al terreno, sino que ,junto con la casa ya existente y la de invitados adyacente, captura el espacio alrededor de un patio nuevo, creando una zona exterior protegida e íntima desde la que disfrutar de un paisaje idílico.

The existing eighteenth-century stone farmhouse, with its wide plank wood flooring, and rustic hearths was appealing to the new inhabitants, but it lacked the modern spaces and amenities they desired to support a contemporary lifestyle.

Das bestehende Bauernhaus aus Stein aus dem achtzehnten Jahrhundert mit einem Boden aus breiten Holzdielen und rustikalen Feuerstellen gefiel den neuen Bewohnern, aber ihnen fehlten moderne Räume und Annehmlichkeiten, die sie sich für einen zeitgemäßen Lifestyle wünschten.

La ferme d'origine, datant du XVIIIe siècle, a plu aux nouveaux habitants avec ses planchers massifs aux larges lattes, mais il lui manquait les espaces et les équipements modernes qu'ils désiraient pour accueillir leur style de vie contemporain.

La granja original de piedra datada en siglo XVIII, con su suelo de anchos tablones de madera y chimeneas rústicas, era atractiva para los nuevos residentes, pero carecía de los espacios e instalaciones modernos que deseaban para llevar un estilo de vida contemporáneo.

New west elevation

New east elevation

New south elevation

New building section

16 ft

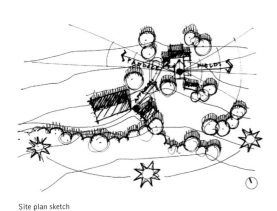

Site plan sketch

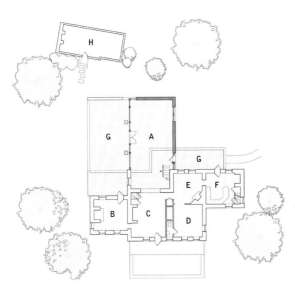

Site plan

A.Existing farmhouse   D.Barn
B.Extension   E.Paddock
C.Guest house   F.Fields

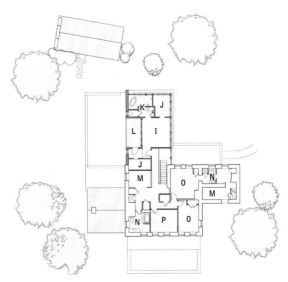

New ground floor plan

A. Family room   I. Master bedroom
B. Playroom   J. Dressing room
C. Living room   K. Master bathroom
D. Dining room   L. Balcony
E. Breakfast room   M. Office
F. Kitchen   N. Bathroom
G. Patio   O. Bedroom
H. Guest house   P. Exercise room

New first floor plan

271

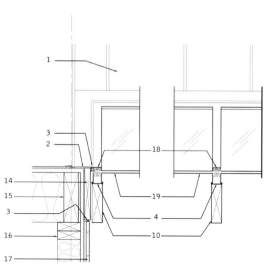

Section detail, sloped glazing

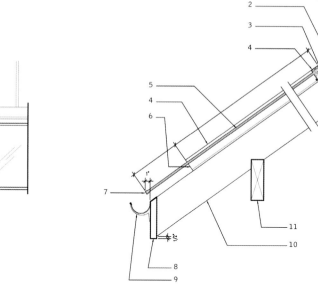

Section detail, sloped glazing

1. Copper roofing
2. Copper flashing
3. Sealant
4. Sloped glazing: manufacturer's standard extruded aluminium head rafter with Kynar finish
5. ½'' laminated glass with 12''cantilever
6. Welded end cap @ aluminium rafter
7. Manufacturer's standard glass edge treatment
8. 2 x cedar fascia
9. Half round copper gutter
10. 3 x 8 cedar framing
11. 3 x 10 cedar beam
12. Tong and groove wood deck
13. 30 lb felt on 1-1/4'' plywood sheathing
14. Wood blocking
15. Sloped Paralam beam per structural drawings
16. 2 x wood framing
17. Clear grade tongue and groove cedar siding on vertical wood furring
18. Manufacturer's standard extruded aluminium cap with Kynar finish
19. ½'' laminated sloped glass

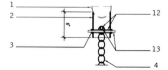

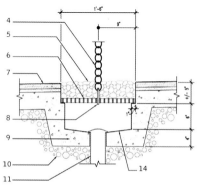

Section detail, rain chain

1. Copper half round gutter
2. Copper outlet tube
3. Secure threaded copper rod with copper hex nut, typical
4. Galvanized steel chain
5. River rock drainage bed
6. Galvanized steel bar grating or catch basin cover, secure to concrete
7. Stone paving on 3/4'' mortar bed
8. Galvanized steel U-bolt
9. Concrete catch basin
10. Gravel drainage fill
11. Yard drain to daylight
12. ¾'' diameter PVC pipe (concealed within outlet tube)
13. ½'' diameter threaded copper rod encased within ¾'' diameter PVC sleeve
14. Slope for positive drainage

SCALE: 0 .5 1 2 FEET

A new entry on the south side of the house was created to replace the original on the north, whose orientation no longer made sense given the winding vehicular approach to the house. Natural materials sympathetic to the existing were used throughout.

An der Südseite des Hauses wurde ein neuer Eingang angelegt, der den alten an der Nordseite ersetzte. Letzterer war nicht mehr sinnvoll, da man das Haus aus dieser Richtung mit dem Auto nur über einen gewundenen Weg erreichen konnte. Es wurden durchweg natürliche Materialien verwendet, die mit den bereits vorhandenen harmonieren.

Une nouvelle entrée du côté sud de la maison a été créée en remplacement de l'originale, côté nord, dont l'orientation n'avait plus de raison d'être étant donné l'aspect sinueux de l'accès à la maison. Des matériaux naturels, en concordance avec ceux d'origine, ont été utilisés pour toute la rénovation.

Se creó una nueva entrada en el lado sur de la casa para reemplazar la original en el norte, cuya orientación ya no tenía sentido dado el sinuoso acceso a la vivienda. En todo el proyecto se utilizaron materiales naturales afines a los existentes.

The size and siting of the addition were restricted by the location of the guesthouse, whilst its scale and simple massing were designed to respect the character and presence of the original structure.

Die Größe und Lage des Anbaus waren durch den Standort des Gästehauses beschränkt und gleichzeitig wurden die Dimensionen und der reine Baukörper so entworfen, dass sie dem Charakter und der Präsenz des ursprünglichen Baus entsprechen.

La taille et l'implantation de l'annexe ont été limitées par l'implantation de la maison d'hôtes, tandis que son échelle et la simplicité de ses volumes ont été conçues pour respecter le caractère et la présence de la structure d'origine.

La ubicación de la casa de invitados limitaba el tamaño y emplazamiento de la ampliación. Su escala y sencilla volumetría se diseñaron para respetar el carácter y presencia de la estructura original.

Creating a strong visual connection to the site and maximising natural light through orientation were high priorities. Glass was used to manipulate light and control views, but also, more formally, as a connector between old and new.

Hohe Prioritäten waren die Schaffung einer visuellen Verbindung zum Grundstück und die Maximierung natürlichen Lichts durch die Ausrichtung. Es wurde Glas verwendet, um Licht gezielt einzusetzen und die Ausblicke zu steuern, aber auch um, in formaler Hinsicht, eine Verbindung zwischen Alt und Neu zu kreieren.

La création d'une forte connexion visuelle avec le site et l'optimisation de la lumière naturelle par le biais de l'orientation étaient des priorités absolues. Le verre a été utilisé pour manipuler la lumière et contrôler les points de vue, mais également, dans une optique plus conceptuelle, en tant que trait d'union entre l'ancien et le nouveau.

Se estableció como prioridad la creación de una fuerte conexión visual con el paisaje colindante y la maximización de la luz natural en base a la orientación. El cristal se usó para manipular la luz y controlar las vistas y también, de manera más formal, como un conector entre lo antiguo y lo nuevo.

COPPER EXTENSION
A space odyssey

MARIAKERKE, BELGIUM

TOTAL BUILDING AREA: 2368 sq ft – 220 m²
EXTENSION AREA: 355 sq ft – 33 m² // 15% of total area

"The new building volume seems to have landed on the site as a sort of retro-futuristic capsule reminiscent of the exploits of Jules Verne; (...) a cocktail of science fiction and nostalgia." This is how the architects describe their design for the extension of an old farmhouse, which had already been extended with a glazed volume. The new design approach is anything but inconspicuous. It stands out as a clear, readable volume with a strong identity and no contextual reference. At the same time, it gives new coherence to the existing structures, creating a striking, yet sensible composition.

« Le volume du nouveau bâtiment semble avoir atterri sur le site comme une sorte de capsule rétro-futuriste évocatrice des exploits de Jules Verne ; (...) un cocktail de science fiction et de nostalgie ». C'est ainsi que les architectes décrivent leur design pour l'extension d'une ancienne ferme qui avait déjà été agrandie par le biais d'un volume vitré. Cette nouvelle approche conceptuelle n'a rien de circonspect. Elle se démarque en tant que volume clair, lisible doté d'une forte identité et dénué de référence contextuelle. En même temps, elle donne une nouvelle cohérence aux structures existantes en créant une composition surprenante, mais rationnelle.

„Der neue Gebäudeteil scheint als eine Art retro-futuristische Kapsel auf dem Grundstück gelandet zu sein, die an die Abenteuer von Jules Verne erinnert; (...) eine Mischung aus Science Fiction und Nostalgie". So beschreiben die Architekten ihr Design für den Anbau eines alten Bauernhauses, das bereits mit einem verglasten Anbau erweitert worden war. Das neue Design ist alles andere als unauffällig. Der Anbau zeichnet sich als klarer, lesbarer Gebäudeteil mit einer starken Identität ohne kontextbezogene Referenzen aus. Gleichzeitig setzt es die bestehenden Gebäude in einen neuen Zusammenhang und schafft damit eine markante, aber stimmige Komposition.

"El volumen del nuevo edificio parece haber aterrizado en el terreno como una especie de cápsula retrofuturista, con reminiscencias de las proezas de Julio Verne; (...) una combinación de ciencia ficción y nostalgia". Así describen los arquitectos su diseño para la ampliación de una granja antigua, a la que ya se había añadido un volumen acristalado. Un diseño que no pasa desapercibido. Se yergue como un volumen claro y comprensible, con una gran identidad y sin referencias contextuales. Al mismo tiempo, da coherencia a las estructuras existentes, creando una composición tan llamativa como llena de sentido.

The property, situated at the back of a plot, is formed by a typical old farmhouse and an extension dating from the nineties with a distinct architecture consisting of a fully glazed curved façade and parallel roofs sloping in two opposite directions.

Cette propriété, située à l'arrière d'un terrain, est composée d'une ferme typique et d'une extension datant des années 90 avec une architecture particulière constituée d'une façade courbe complètement vitrée et de toits parallèles aux pentes opposées.

Das Objekt, das sich im hinteren Teil des Grundstücks befindet, besteht aus einem typischen alten Bauernhaus und einem Anbau aus den neunziger Jahren, der eine markante Architektur aufweist. Er besteht aus einer vollständig verglasten geschwungenen Fassade und hat parallele Dachflächen, die sich in entgegengesetzte Richtungen neigen.

La propiedad, situada en la parte trasera del terreno, está formada por una antigua y típica granja y una ampliación realizada en la década de los noventa, con un estilo distinto. Esta extensión incluye una fachada curva completamente acristalada y tejados paralelos que se inclinan en dos direcciones opuestas.

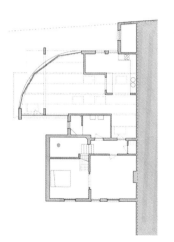

Original ground floor plan

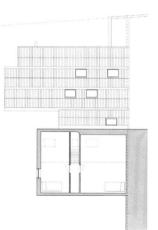

Original first floor plan

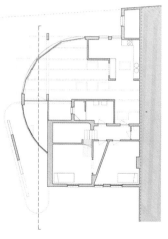

New ground floor plan

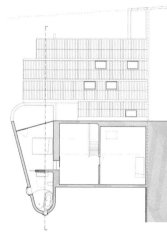

New first floor plan

0   5m

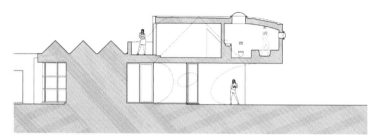

Section through extension

0   5m

The extension creates a sheltered entry porch framed by the new glazed entrance—formed by the continuation of the curved façade— and a sculptural copper-clad leg.

Der Anbau lässt eine geschützte Veranda entstehen, die von dem neuen verglasten Eingang – der durch die Fortführung der geschwungenen Fassade gebildet wird – und einer skulpturalen, mit Kupfer verkleideten Stütze eingerahmt wird.

L'extension crée un porche encadré par la nouvelle entrée vitrée – que forme la continuité de la façade incurvée – et un jambage monumental habillé de cuivre.

La extensión crea un porche cerrado enmarcado por la nueva entrada acristalada –formada por la continuación de la fachada curva– y un escultural pie revestido en cobre.

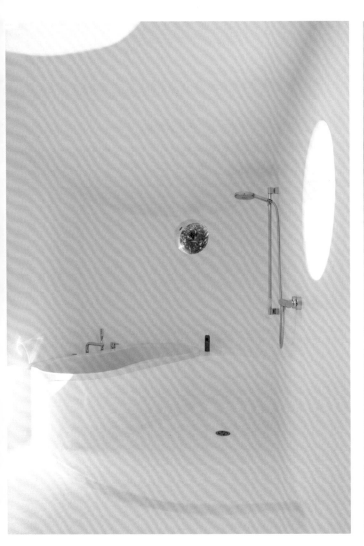

The extension, which contains a new bedroom with a balcony and a bathroom, is accessed via a multipurpose room on the first floor of the farmhouse.

Der Anbau, der ein neues Schlafzimmer mit einem Balkon und einem Badezimmer beherbergt, kann über einen Mehrzweckraum im Erdgeschoss des Bauernhauses erreicht werden.

On accède à cette extension, qui contient une nouvelle chambre donnant sur un balcon et une salle d'eau, par le biais d'une pièce multifonctionnelle au premier étage de la ferme.

El nuevo espacio alberga un dormitorio con balcón y un baño. Se accede a estas dependencias desde una sala multiusos en la primera planta de la granja.

BORD-DU-LAC HOUSE

Multigenerational home

DORVAL, QUÉBEC, CANADA

TOTAL BUILDING AREA: 10353 sq ft – 962 m^2
EXTENSION AREA: 5606 sq ft – 521 m^2 // 54.1% of total area

A 200-year-old Quebec stone cottage was remodelled and extended with a striking Corten steel and glass construction. The design approach reconciles a contemporary architectural language to the old home. The functional program, which accommodates a four-generation family, and the juxtaposition of contrasting structures are aimed at expressing the passage of time. The result highlights the old stone building as a living entity that can accommodate changes without losing its original character, whilst coexisting harmoniously with the new addition.

Un cottage Québécois en pierre vieux de deux cents ans a été remanié et doté d'une impressionnante extension en verre et acier Corten. Dans son approche, ce design concilie l'ancien bâtiment et un langage architectural contemporain. Un programme fonctionnel, qui prend en compte quatre générations de la même famille, et la juxtaposition de structures contrastées, visent à évoquer le passage du temps. Ce qui permet au vieux bâtiment d'être mis en valeur en tant qu'entité vivante capable de s'adapter aux changements sans perdre de son caractère original, tout en coexistant harmonieusement avec les éléments ajoutés.

Ein 200 Jahre altes Natursteinhaus in Quebec wurde umgebaut und mit einem markanten Anbau aus Cortenstahl und Glas erweitert. Das Design vereint eine zeitgenössische Architektursprache auf harmonische Weise mit dem alten Gebäude. Das Funktionsprogramm für eine Familie mit vier Generationen und die Nebeneinanderstellung von kontrastierenden Bauten sollen den Lauf der Zeit ausdrücken. Das Ergebnis lässt das alte Steinhaus lebendig erscheinen: Es ist in der Lage, Änderungen anzunehmen, ohne dabei seinen ursprünglichen Charakter zu verlieren, und neben dem neuen Anbau harmonisch zu koexistieren.

Una casa de piedra de doscientos años en Quebec fue remodelada y ampliada con una estructura sorprendente de acero Corten y cristal. El enfoque de diseño reconcilia el lenguaje arquitectónico contemporáneo con la vieja casa. El programa funcional, que da cabida a una familia de cuatro generaciones y la yuxtaposición de estructuras que contrastan, están dirigidos a expresar el paso del tiempo. El resultado pone de relieve la antigua construcción de piedra como una entidad viva que puede adaptarse a los cambios sin perder su carácter original, siempre que coexista en armonía con la nueva ampliación.

HENRI CLEINGE ARCHITECT

The original structure once had the main entrance facing a river, where the old road was. Over time, a new road was built on the backside of the house, which, with the extension work, became the front.

Der Haupteingang des ursprünglichen Gebäudes befand sich dort, wo die alte Straße verlief, und war einem Fluss zugewandt. Im Laufe der Zeit wurde eine neue Straße an der Hinterseite des Hauses gebaut, die mit den Ausbauarbeiten zur Vorderseite wurde.

Dans la structure initiale, l'entrée principale donnait sur une rivière, où passait l'ancienne route. Quelques temps plus tard, une nouvelle route a été construite à l'arrière de la maison qui, avec la nouvelle extension, est devenue l'avant.

La estructura original tenía la entrada principal frente a un río, donde estaba la antigua carretera. Con el tiempo, se construyó un nuevo acceso en la parte trasera de la casa que, con la obra de extensión, se convirtió en la parte delantera.

Original building's east elevation

Original building's west elevation

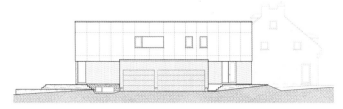

Extension's east elevation

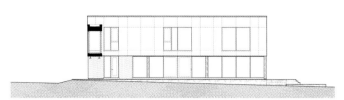

Extension's west elevation

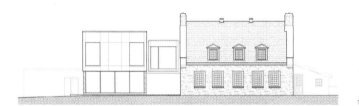

Extension's north elevation

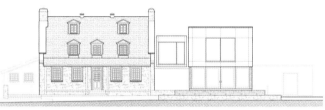

Extension's south elevation

3 15   30   60 ft

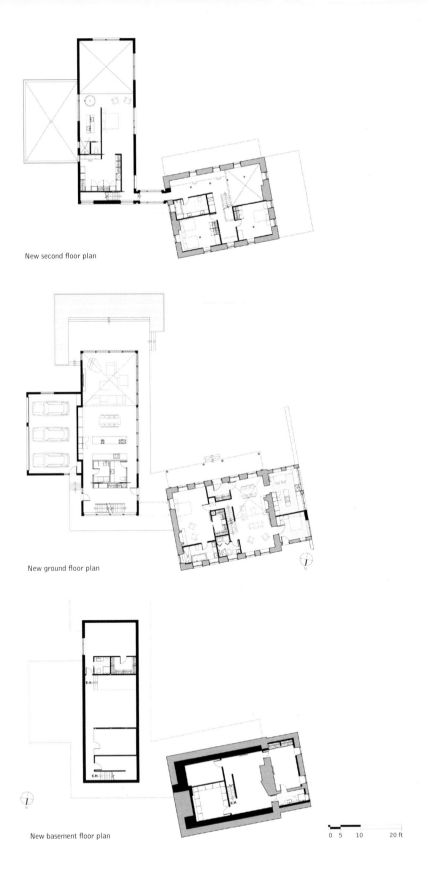

New second floor plan

New ground floor plan

New basement floor plan

0   5   10   20 ft

The contemporary elements in the old house such as the modern kitchen equipment and finishes coexist with the stone walls and the ceiling wood beams, bringing together tradition and modern construction in creative synergy.

Die zeitgenössischen Elemente im alten Haus, wie die moderne Küchenausstattung und die modernen Oberflächen, koexistieren mit den Steinwänden und den Dachbalken aus Holz. So werden Tradition und Moderne in einem kreativen Zusammenspiel vereint.

Les éléments contemporains de la vieille maison tels que le matériel culinaire et les finitions modernes coexistent avec les murs de pierre et les poutres en bois, la tradition et la construction moderne s'associent en une synergie créatrice.

Los elementos contemporáneos de la vieja casa, tales como los acabados y los modernos accesorios de la cocina, coexisten con las paredes de piedra y las vigas de madera del techo, reuniendo así la tradición y la construcción moderna en una sinergia creativa.

CLIFFS IMPASSE

Beyond the walls

SENNEVILLE-SUR-FÉCAMP, FRANCE

TOTAL BUILDING AREA: 1184 sq ft – 110 m^2
EXTENSION AREA: 646 sq ft – 60 m^2 // 54.5% of total area

The extension of an old rural stone house explores the idea of inserting new buildings into a landscape and their compatibility with existing structures. A glazed entry hall eases the transition between the house and a contemporary wooden extension, consisting of a black plywood box with no formal association with the existing building. The extension provides space for a garage on the ground floor and a reading room on the upper floor. Inserted into the existing house, a small staircase leads to a space high above the ground, which provides an escape from every known frame of reference, and offers an environment that promotes reflection and creativity.

L'extension d'une ancienne maison de campagne en pierre explore l'idée d'insérer de nouveaux bâtiments dans un paysage et leur compatibilité avec les structures existantes. Un hall d'entrée vitré facilite la transition entre la maison et une extension contemporaine en bois, faite d'une « boîte » de contreplaqué sans association formelle avec le bâtiment existant. Cet ajout procure de l'espace pour un garage au rez-de-chaussée et une salle de lecture à l'étage supérieur. Inséré dans la maison existante, un petit escalier mène à un espace en hauteur qui permet d'échapper à toute forme de cadre de références, et offre un environnement propice à la réflexion et à la créativité.

Die Erweiterung eines alten ländlichen Steinhauses geht dem Konzept nach, neue Gebäude und ihre Kompatibilität mit bestehenden Bauten in eine Landschaft einzufügen. Der verglaste Eingangsbereich lockert den Übergang zwischen dem Haus und einem modernen Anbau aus Holz auf. Bei dem Anbau handelt es sich um einen Kastenbau aus schwarzem Schichtholz, der keine formale Verbindung zu dem bestehenden Gebäude aufweist. Er bietet Platz für eine Garage im Erdgeschoss und einen Leseraum im Obergeschoss. Eine kleine Treppe, die in das bestehende Haus eingebaut wurde, führt zu einem hoch gelegenen Raum, in dem die Bewohner allen bekannten Bezugsrahmen entfliehen können. Die Umgebung dieses Raums fördert außerdem die Reflexion und die Kreativität.

El anexo de una antigua casa rural explora la idea de insertar nuevos edificios en un paisaje y su compatibilidad con estructuras existentes. Una entrada acristalada facilita la transición entre la casa y el anexo de madera contemporáneo, que está formado por una caja de madera contrachapada negra sin asociación directa con el edificio existente. Esta ampliación proporciona el espacio para un garaje en la planta baja y una biblioteca en la planta superior. Desde la vivienda original, una pequeña escalera conduce a un espacio elevado que proporciona un escape a cualquier escala de referencia y ofrece un entorno que invita a la reflexión y a la creatividad.

ZIEGLER ANTONIN ARCHITECTE

Photos © Antonin Ziegler

For the occupants of this small country house, the space felt cramped within its massive stone walls. They also didn't feel isolated enough, something they longed to better enjoy their reading and writing.

Les occupants de cette petite maison de campagne trouvaient que l'espace paraissait étriqué à l'intérieur des épais murs de pierre. Ils avaient aussi l'impression de ne pas être suffisamment isolés, condition à laquelle ils tenaient pour pouvoir mieux profiter de leurs activités de lecture et d'écriture.

Für die Bewohner dieses kleinen Landhauses waren die Platzverhältnisse innerhalb der massiven Steinmauern beengt. Außerdem fühlten sie sich nicht isoliert genug, was sie sich wünschten, um dem Lesen und Schreiben besser nachgehen zu können.

Los habitantes de esta pequeña casa de campo sentían que el espacio se contraía dentro de sus grandes muros de piedra. Tampoco se sentían suficientemente aislados, algo que anhelaban para disfrutar completamente de la lectura y escritura.

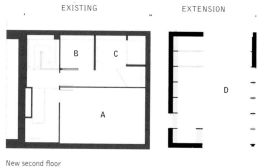

New second floor

A. Bedroom   C. Bathroom
B. Laundry room D. Library

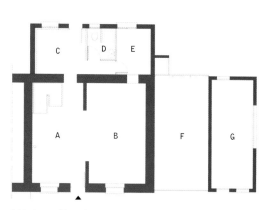

Original ground floor plan

A. Dining room   E. Laundry room
B. Living room   F. Garage
C. Kitchen   G. Storage room
D. Bathroom

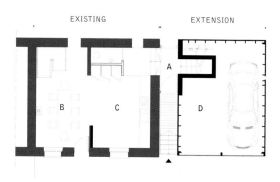

New ground floor plan

A. Entrance   C. Kitchen
B. Dining room D. Garage

0 1 2   5

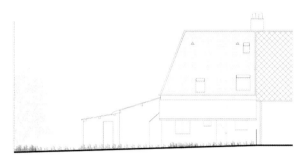

Original south-west building elevation

Original north-east building elevation

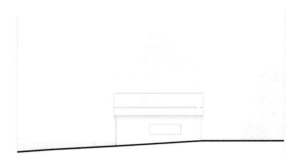

Original north-west building elevation

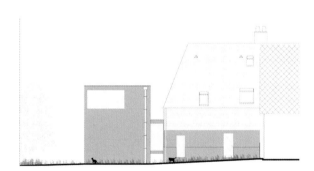

New south-west elevation

New north-west elevation

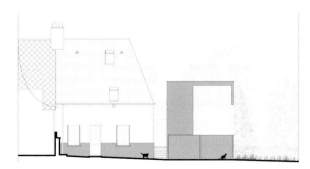

New north-east elevation

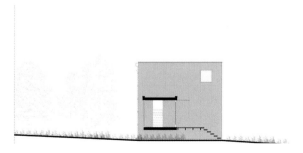

Section through entrance, facing extension

0   1   2   5   N

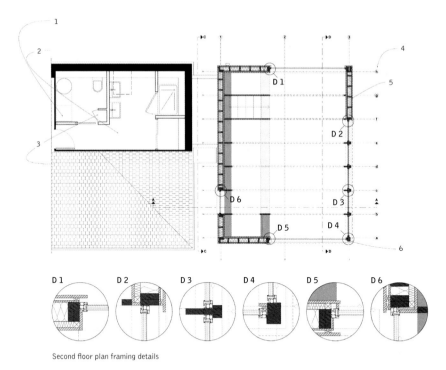

1. Mechanically controlled ventilation, single flow self-adjustment in isolated service duct (acoustic insulation) + access hatch
2. Fitting of a bathroom + laundry room on second floor
   - Partitioning + equipment + electricity
   - Flooring: to be varnished
   - Wall ceramic tile (over moisture-resistant plasterboard), full height in shower and at washbasins
3. Mechanically controlled ventilation, single flow self-adjustment (roof exit), and access hatch at highest point
   - Exposed ducts in rigid, flat and rectangular conduits
4. Structural floor framing, 90 cm on centre
5. - 22 mm thick exterior grade okoume plywood panels
   - Black pine tar protection layer
   - 20 x 45 mm battens
   - Waterproof membrane
   - 12 mm OSB
   - 45 x 145 mm uprights
6. Sheet metal, lacquered in RAL to match building finish over wood post

Exterior cladding – wall caps and other lacquered aluminium parts painted in RAL 9005 (unless otherwise noted)

Second floor plan framing details

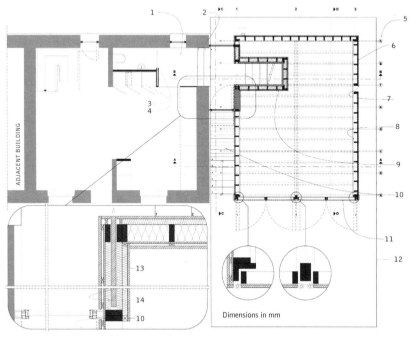

Ground floor plan framing details

1. Subfloor
   - 12 mm okoume plywood flooring
   - Clear wood stain
2. Door framing in the continuity of existing walls and ceilings
3. Kitchen equipment to be determined
4. Plasterboard + pocket door
5. Structural floor framing, 90 cm on centre
6. - 22 mm thick exterior grade okoume plywood panels
   - Black pine tar protection layer
   - 20 x 45 mm battens
   - Waterproof membrane
   - 12 mm OSB
   - 45 x 145 mm uprights
7. Vertical opening through ground and second floor
8. Bituminous coating (black) on all wall faces (including tops)
9. Staircase wood frame
   - 12 mm okoume plywood flooring
   - Transparent wood stain
   - Sound insulation 30 mm
   - 18 mm OSB wall sheathing
   - Vapour barrier
   - 225 x 75 mm stringers
   - Insulation 200 mm
   - Support beam 25 x 50
   - 6 mm OSB subfloor
   - Riser = 19 cm
   - Tread = 31 cm

10. Wood decking (1 cm spaces between boards)
    - Non-slip wood slats
    - Lay of the slats perpendicular to existing wall
11. Double-leaf garage door
    - Finish to match exterior wall finish
    - Door face to be flush with face of building
12. Black basalt gravel over stabilizing drainage slab
13. - 22 mm thick interior grade okoume plywood panels
    - Black pine tar protection layer
    - 20 x 45 mm battens
    - Waterproof membrane
    - 12 mm OSB
    - 45 x 145 mm uprights
    - Insulation 150 mm
    - Pocket door
    - 45 x 45 mm uprights
    - Waterproof membrane
    - Exterior OSB panel
14. Pocket door
    - 22 mm thick exterior grade okoume plywood panels
    - Black pine tar protection layer
    - 22 mm thick interior okoume plywood panel
    - Clear wood stain

Exterior cladding – wall caps and other lacquered aluminium parts painted in RAL 9005 (unless otherwise noted)

Dimensions in mm

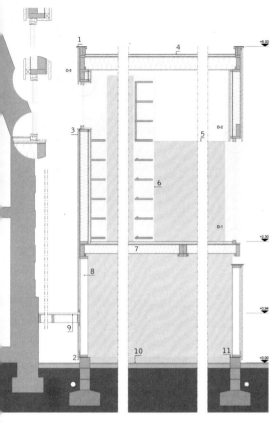

Detail section AA

1. Lacquered wall cap, 30 mm max. on wall face
2. Lower part of the exterior wall at 50 mm above ground max. (constant height to be respected on all exterior wall)
3. - 22 mm thick exterior grade okoume plywood panels
   - Black pine tar protection layer
   - 20 x 45 mm battens
   - Waterproof membrane
   - 12 mm OSB
   - 45 x 145 mm uprights
   - Insulation 150 mm
   - Vapour barrier
   - 45 x 45 uprights
   - Insulation 50 mm
   - 22 mm thick interior okoume plywood panel
   - Clear wood stain
4. Wood framing of roof terrace
   - Waterproofing
   - 40 mm insulating panel
   - Vapour barrier
   - 21 mm OSB
   - 225 x 75 panels
   - 200 mm insulation
   - 22 mm thick interior okoume plywood panel
5. Alignment to be respected
6. Decorative wooden structure in planed spruce
   - Framing at 90 cm on centre
   - 45 x 400 mm sections (vertical elements) and 30 x 340 mm sections (horizontal sections)
7. Wood floor framing
   - 12 mm okoume plywood flooring
   - Clear wood stain
   - Sound insulation 30 mm
   - 18 mm OSB wall sheathing
   - Vapour barrier
   - 225 x 75 panels
   - 200 mm insulation
   - 25 x 50 support beam
   - 6 mm OSB subfloor
8. - 22 mm thick exterior grade okoume plywood panels
   - Black pine tar protection layer
   - 20 x 45 mm battens
   - Waterproof membrane
   - 12 mm OSB
   - 45 x 145 mm uprights
9. Wood decking (1 cm spaces between boards)
   - Non-slip wood slats
   - Lay of the slats perpendicular to existing wall
10. Black basalt gravel over stabilizing drainage slab
11. Bituminous coating (black) on all wall faces (including tops)

Exterior cladding – wall caps and other lacquered aluminium parts painted in RAL 9005 (unless otherwise noted)

Detail section BB

1. Door framing in the continuity of existing walls and ceilings
2. - Subfloor
   - 12 mm okoume plywood flooring
   - Clear wood stain
3. - 22 mm thick exterior grade okoume plywood panels
   - Black pine tar protection layer
   - 20 x 45 mm battens
   - Waterproof membrane
   - 12 mm OSB
   - 45 x 145 mm uprights
   - Insulation 150 mm
   - Vapour barrier
   - 45 x 45 uprights
   - Insulation 50 mm
   - 22 mm thick interior okoume plywood panel
   - Clear wood stain
4. Wood framing of roof terrace
   - Waterproofing
   - 40 mm insulating panel
   - Vapour barrier
   - 21 mm OSB
   - 225 x 75 panels
   - 200 mm insulation
   - 22 mm thick interior okoume plywood panel
   - Clear wood stain
5. Waterproof steel roof
   - Waterproofing
   - 200 mm insulation
   - Vapour barrier
   - Lacquered corrugated metal sheet
6. - Decorative wooden structure in planed spruce
   - Framing at 90 cm on centre
   - 45 x 400 mm sections (vertical elements) and 30 x 340 mm sections (horizontal sections)
7. Library sliding ladder
8. Alignment to be respected (guardrail/shelf/lintel)
9. Staircase wood frame
   - 12 mm okoume plywood flooring
   - Transparent wood stain
   - Sound insulation 30 mm
   - 18 mm OSB wall sheathing
   - Vapour barrier
   - 225 x 75 mm stringers
   - Insulation 200 mm
   - Support beam 25 x 50
   - 6 mm OSB subfloor
   - Riser = 19 cm
   - Tread = 31 cm
10. Pocket door
    - 22 mm thick exterior grade okoume plywood panels
    - Black pine tar protection layer
    - 22 mm thick interior okoume plywood panel
    - Clear wood stain
11. Lower part of the exterior wall at 50 mm above ground max. (constant height to be respected on all exterior wall)
12. Bituminous coating (black) on all wall faces (including tops)
13. Black basalt gravel over stabilizing drainage slab

Exterior cladding – wall caps and other lacquered aluminium parts painted in RAL 9005 (unless otherwise noted)

Open on three sides, the interior space is exposed to the views, like a book opened to the landscape. Its open character is complemented by the warmth bought by the wooden surfaces and the lighting.

Der auf drei Seiten geöffnete Innenraum bietet großartige Ausblicke, wie ein Buch, das sich der Landschaft öffnet. Der offene Charakter wird durch eine gemütliche Atmosphäre ergänzt, die durch Holzoberflächen und das Licht entstehen.

Sur trois faces, l'espace intérieur est livré aux vues extérieures, comme un livre ouvert sur le paysage. Cette qualité est complétée par l'aspect chaleureux des surfaces de bois et de l'éclairage.

Abierto por tres lados, el espacio interior se muestra a la vistas, como un libro expuesto al paisaje. Su carácter abierto se complementa con la calidez que aportan las superficies de madera y la iluminación.

Beyond offering views and providing a place for evasion, the space also creates a new relationship with the surrounding natural landscape in a way that the original house can't offer.

Der Raum bietet nicht nur Ausblicke und eine Rückzugsmöglichkeit, sondern kreiert eine neue Beziehung zu der umliegenden Naturlandschaft, die das ursprüngliche Haus auf diese Weise nicht bieten kann.

Au-delà du fait qu'il apporte des vues et un lieu d'évasion, cet espace crée également une relation nouvelle avec le paysage naturel environnant que la maison d'origine ne peut égaler.

Además de ofrecer grandes vistas y un lugar para evadirse, el anexo también crea una nueva relación con el paisaje que la rodea que la casa original no podía ofrecer.

KENWORTHY HOUSE

Rethinking the family home

LONDON, UNITED KINGDOM

TOTAL BUILDING AREA: 1916 sq ft – 178 m²
EXTENSION AREA: 1108 sq ft – 103 m² // 58% of total area

An existing narrow closet wing was demolished and rebuilt as a lightweight, highly insulated timber frame construction. A double height glazed screen indicates the new entry point and gives a clear visual separation between the old part of the house and the new. A loft conversion clad in the same material completes the extension of the accommodation. The finished building provides the family with spacious, bright bedrooms; a large family kitchen with breakfast and dining area that opens up to the garden; and a striking, modern piece of architecture that complements the existing building.

Une étroite extension arrière d'origine a été démolie et reconstruite dans une version légère, avec une ossature en bois et une très bonne isolation. Une panneau vitré en double hauteur indique le nouveau point d'accès et offre une séparation visuelle claire entre l'ancienne partie de la maison et la nouvelle. L'aménagement des combles, parés des mêmes matériaux, complète l'extension de ce logement. Le bâtiment terminé procure à la famille des chambres spacieuses et claires ; une grande cuisine familiale comprenant table de petit déjeuner et salle-à-manger qui s'ouvre sur le jardin ; et un exemple saisissant d'architecture moderne qui complète le bâtiment d'origine.

Ein bestehender enger Anbau wurde abgerissen und als sehr gut isolierter Leichtbau mit Holzrahmen neu gebaut. Eine verglaste Wand mit doppelter Raumhöhe markiert den neuen Eingang und stellt eine deutliche visuelle Trennung zwischen dem alten und dem neuen Teil des Hauses dar. Ein mit dem gleichen Material verkleideter Dachgeschossausbau rundet die Erweiterung des Hauses ab. Das fertiggestellte Gebäude bietet der Familie geräumige, helle Schlafzimmer, eine große Familienküche mit Essbereich, die sich zum Garten öffnet, und ein markantes, modernes architektonisches Werk, das das bestehende Gebäude ergänzt.

Se demolió una estrecha ampliación existente en la parte de atrás y se erigió de nuevo como una construcción ligera, que destaca por el uso de la madera y su gran aislamiento. Una apertura de cristal a doble altura indica el nuevo punto de entrada y otorga una clara separación entre la parte antigua y la nueva de la casa. La transformación de la buhardilla recubierta del mismo material completa la ampliación de la vivienda. El edificio resultante proporciona a la familia dormitorios espaciosos y luminosos, una gran cocina con zona de desayuno y un comedor abierto al jardín; una pieza arquitectónica, moderna y llamativa que complementa el edificio original.

CHRIS DYSON ARCHITECTS

The entrance to the house was relocated to the centre of the plan, providing a dramatic entry into the heart of the house, whilst freeing up the previous entry position to be used as an entry-level water closet.

Der Eingang zum Haus wurde in die Mitte des Objekts verlegt, wodurch ein spektakulärer Zugang zum Herzen des Hauses entstanden ist. Dort, wo sich zuvor der Eingang befand, wurde Platz für ein WC auf der Eingangsebene geschaffen.

L'entrée de la maison a été transférée au centre du plan, ce qui produit un accès saisissant au cœur de la maison, tout en libérant l'emplacement de la précédente pour un cabinet de toilette au niveau de l'entrée.

La entrada se reubicó en el centro del plano para conseguir un espectacular acceso al corazón de la vivienda, a la vez que libera la antigua entrada para convertirse en un baño en la planta baja.

The extension and the loft are clad with charred cedar boards, which beautifully complement the Victorian brickwork of the surrounding context and give the extension a firm legibility as a modern intervention.

Die Erweiterung und das Dachgeschoss sind mit verkohlten Zedernholzbrettern verkleidet, die das viktorianische Mauerwerk des umgebenden Kontexts ergänzen und den Anbau deutlich als modernen architektonischen Eingriff erkennbar machen.

L'extension et les combles sont bardés de cèdre brûlé, ce qui s'accorde joliment avec les parements de brique victoriens du contexte environnant et donne à la construction une franche lisibilité en tant qu'intervention moderne.

La ampliación y la buhardilla están revestidas con placas de madera de cedro oscuro, que complementan el ladrillo victoriano que lo rodea y le da a la ampliación la legitimidad de una intervención moderna.

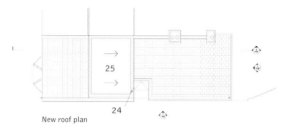

New roof plan

25

24

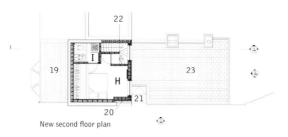

New second floor plan

22

19   I

23

H

21

20

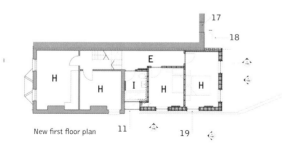

New first floor plan

17

18

H

H   I   H   H

E

11   19

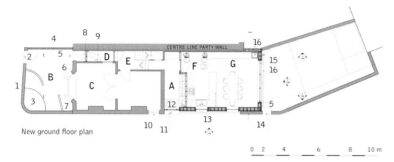

New ground floor plan

8   9

4

CENTRE LINE PARTY WALL   16

2   5

6   D   E   15

1   B   16

A

C   F   G

3   7

12   5

10   11   13   14

A. Entrance
B. Garden
C. Living room
D. Powder room
E. Hall
F. Study area
G. Kitchen/dining area
H. Bedroom
I. Bathroom

1. 1100 high brick wall
2. Gate
3. Planting
4. 950 high brick wall
5. New drainage connections,
   new manhole location to be
   determined on site
6. Gas meter
7. Rainwater pipe
8. Retained front door form.
   New insulated studwork
9. New WC
10. Retained sash window and
    lintel in new opening

11. Glazed entrance screen
12. Void above
13. Existing garden wall
    partially rebuilt.
    New insulated timber
    weatherboard set behind
14. Existing garden door
15. Aluminium folding door
    system
16. Slot drain
17. Neighbouring window
18. 45 degrees line from centre
19. Existing slate roof
20. Timber weatherboard wall
21. Glazed roof
22. Party wall raised in brick
    to allow neighbour to
    construct loft extension
23. Artificial slate roof
24. Concealed downpipe
    discharging into new
    concealed gutter
25. GRP flat roof to fall
    toward parapet

0   2   4   6   8   10 m

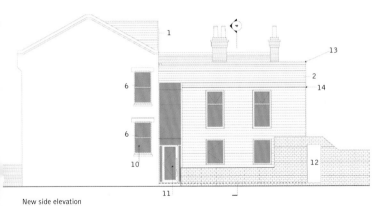

New side elevation

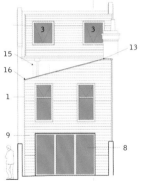

New rear elevation

1. Charred cedar timber weatherboarding
2. Artificial slate
3. PPC aluminium framed window
4. Double glazed panel
5. Glazed entrance screen
6. Reused sliding sash window
7. Existing garden wall
8. Aluminium bifold door
9. Painted render
10. Lower panes to be covered with translucent film
11. Lower area of glass to be translucent/obscure
12. Existing garden door repainted
13. Extension below existing eaves line
14. Concealed gutter detail
15. Existing window opening filled and rendered
16. Minimal flashing to edge of timber

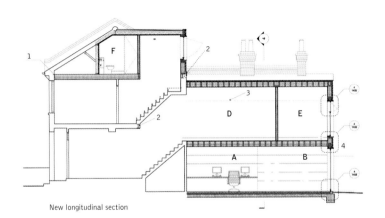

New longitudinal section

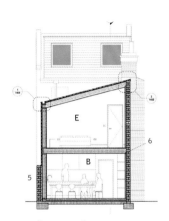

New cross section

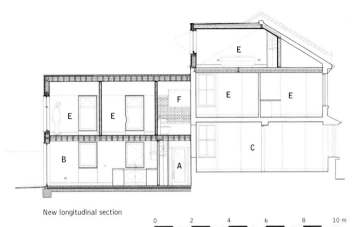

New longitudinal section

A. Study area
B. Kitchen/dining room
C. Living room
D. Hallway
E. Bedroom
F. Bathroom

1. New floor joists to bear on heavy duty joist hangers subject to suitability of existing lintels
2. Steel beam to structural engineer's specification
3. Ceiling at lowest level
4. Structural timber lintel 2 No 250 x 50
5. Existing wall rebuilt on new footing
6. New floor joists to bear on heavy duty joist hangers

0   2   4   6   8   10 m

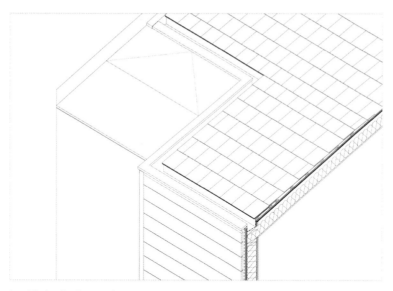

Isometric view of roof construction

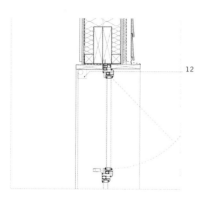

12

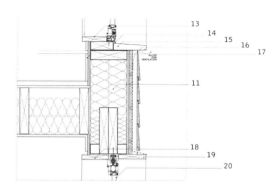

13
14
15 16
17

11

18
19
20

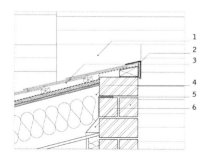

1
2
3
4
5
6

Ridge detail

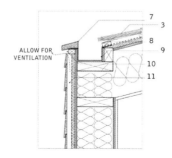

ALLOW FOR
VENTILATION

7
3
8
9
10
11

Concealed gutter detail

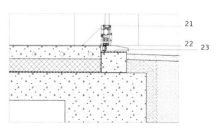

21
22 23

Garden door and window details

1. Code 4 lead flashing to perimeter chased into mortar joint 150 mm above roof level
2. Code 4 lead flashing drip detail over fascia
3. - Marley eternity slates
   - Tanalised SW battens
   - Proclima Solitex WA breather membrane
   - 18 mm WBP plywood
   - 165 mm Celotex XR4000 between rafters
   - Proclima intrlloplus VCL
   - 12.5 mm plasterboard, skim finish
4. Wrap rafters ends in DPC
5. Reclaimed brick party wall extension tied back to existing with starter bars
6. Heavy duty joist hangers built into wall
7. Solid charred cedar coping
8. Breather membrane lapped into gutter
9. Code 4 lead formed gutter on WBP plywood

10. Insect closing ventilated cavity
11. - Charred cedar cladding fixed to battens with sheradised hidden head annular ring shank nails
    - Tanalised SW battens forming ventilated cavity closed top and bottom with insect mesh
    - Proclima Solitex WA breather membrane
    - 25 mm Celotex FR5000 mechanically fixed
    - WBP plywood sheathing
    - Celotex FR4000 between studs
    - Proclima Intelloplus VCL
    - 12 mm plywood
    - 12.5 mm wallboard, skim finish
12. Roller blind fitting
13. Natural cedar internal reveal
14. Silicone seal

15. Natural cedar sill with drip throat cut breather membrane lapped underneath
16. Insect mesh
17. MDF skirting
18. Natural cedar internal reveal, broken around door fixing
19. Natural cedar reveal, breather membrane lapped over top
20. Bifolding timber door
21. - 3 mm poured resin
    - 70 mm screed with UFH heating
    - Isolating membrane
    - Bituthene PDM
    - Slab to engineers spec
22. Bituthene DPM lapped under door threshold
23. Gravel external finish

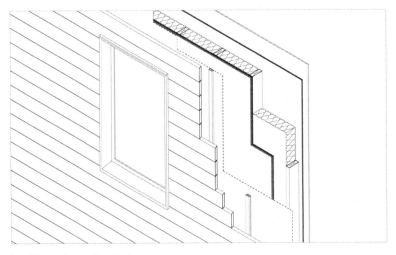

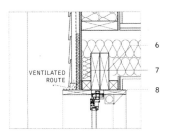

VENTILATED ROUTE

6
7
8

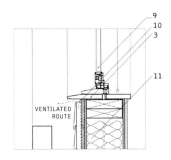

VENTILATED ROUTE

9
10
3
11

Isometric view of new wall construction

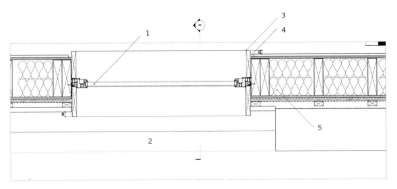

3
4
1
5
2

Typical window plan detail

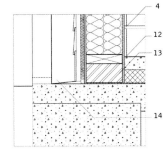

4
12
13
14

Window section detail

1. PPC aluminium double glazed window
2. Garden wall below
3. Natural cedar window sill
4. 15 mm shadow gap trim
5. - Plasterboard, skim finish
   - 12 mm plywood
   - Intelloplus VCL, joints taped
   - Insulation between studs
   - 12 mm WBP plywood
   - Rigid insulation
   - Proclima Solitex WA breather membrane
   - Tanalised SW battens forming ventilated cavity
   - Charred cedar cladding

6. 2/200 x 50 C 24 joists bolted together
7. Lead flashing to top of cedar trim
8. Roller blind system
9. Proprietary aluminium double glazed window
10. Insect mesh to ventilated cavity
11. - Charred cedar cladding fixed to battens with sheradised hidden head annular ring shank nails
    - Tanalised SW battens forming ventilated cavity closed top and bottom with insect mesh
    - Proclima Solitex WA breather membrane
    - 25 mm Celotex FR5000 Mechanically fixed

   - WBP plywood sheathing
   - Celotex FR4000 between studs
   - Proclima Intelloplus VCL
   - 12 mm plywood
   - 12.5 mm plasterboard, skim finish
13. - 3 mm resin floor
    - 70 mm screed with UFH pipes
    - 60 mm insulation
    - Bituthene DPM
    - Structural RC slab
14. Weep holes to base of wall and code 4 lead flashing weathered under base of timber cladding

On the upper floor, the ceiling in the rooms follows the pitch of the roof, giving the spaces additional height and volume. Large format windows flood the rooms with light.

Im Obergeschoss folgen die Zimmerdecken der Dachschräge, was den Räumen zusätzliche Höhe und zusätzliches Volumen verleiht. Großformatige Fenster sorgen für lichtdurchflutete Räume.

À l'étage supérieur, le plafond des pièces suit l'inclinaison du toit, ce qui donne aux espaces une hauteur et un volume supplémentaires. Des fenêtres grand format inondent les pièces de lumière.

En el piso superior, el techo de las habitaciones sigue la inclinación del tejado, otorgando a las estancias mayor altura y volumen. Las ventanas de gran tamaño inundan de luz el interior.

C2A
An integration of eras

CHIHUAHUA CITY, MEXICO

TOTAL BUILDING AREA: 3229 sq ft – 300 m²
EXTENSION AREA: 2368 sq ft – 220 m² // 73.5% of total area

The project began with the restoration of an old building with a forty square-meter footprint dating from the early twentieth century. Later, the neighbouring three hundred square-meter property was added to the program, providing space for an extension of the existing old building. This extension was conceived as a series of articulated volumes and a staircase that not only connects the different floor levels of the extension, but also acts as a link between the old and new constructions.

Le projet a débuté avec la réfection d'une vieille maison datant du début du XXe siècle d'une superficie au sol de quarante mètres carrés. Plus tard, la propriété voisine, de trois cents mètres carrés, a été ajoutée au programme, procurant l'espace nécessaire pour une extension du bâtiment existant. Celle-ci a été conçue en une série de volumes articulés et un escalier qui non seulement relie les différents niveaux de l'extension entre eux, mais sert aussi de trait d'union entre l'ancienne et la nouvelle construction.

Das Projekt begann mit der Restaurierung eines alten Gebäudes aus dem frühen zwanzigsten Jahrhundert, das über eine Grundfläche von vierzig Quadratmetern verfügte. Zu einem späteren Zeitpunkt wurde das benachbarte dreihundert Quadratmeter große Grundstück zu dem Programm hinzugefügt, das Platz für eine Erweiterung des bestehenden alten Gebäudes bot. Diese Erweiterung wurde als eine Reihe von miteinander verbundenen Räumen konzipiert. Eine Treppe verbindet die verschiedenen Etagen des Anbaus miteinander, aber dient gleichzeitig auch als Verbindung zwischen dem alten und dem neuen Gebäude.

El proyecto empezó con la restauración de un antiguo edificio de cuarenta metros cuadrados de planta de principios del s. XX. Más adelante, la superficie vecina de trescientos metros cuadrados se añadió al programa, facilitando espacio para una ampliación del edificio existente. Esta extensión se concibió como una serie de volúmenes articulados y una escalera que además de conectar los distintos pisos de la ampliación, también es el nexo de unión entre las construcciones antiguas y nuevas.

The project was originated by a two-storey building in a deteriorated urban environment. This led to a study around the refurbishment of derelict building structures and the exploration of the possibilities of urban regeneration.

Le projet avait pour origine un bâtiment de deux étages dans un environnement urbain en dégradation. Il a mené à une étude sur la réfection de structures bâties dégradées et sur l'exploration des possibilités de régénération urbaine.

Das Projekt begann mit einem zweistöckigen Gebäude in einer städtischen Umgebung, die sich in schlechtem Zustand befand. Dies führte zu einer Untersuchung bezüglich der Sanierung von verfallenen Gebäudestrukturen und der Analyse von Möglichkeiten im Rahmen der städtischen Erneuerung.

El proyecto lo originó un edificio de dos plantas en un entorno urbano deteriorado. Esto llevó a un estudio sobre la remodelación de unas estructuras en ruinas y la exploración de posibilidades de regeneración urbana.

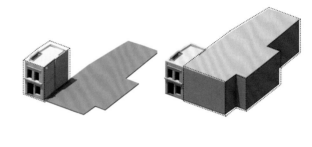

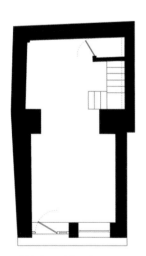

Original ground floor plan

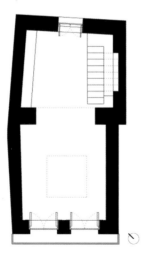

Original second floor plan

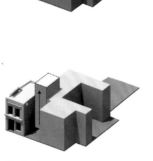
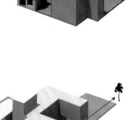

Massing diagrams

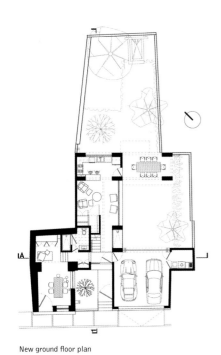

New ground floor plan

New second floor plan

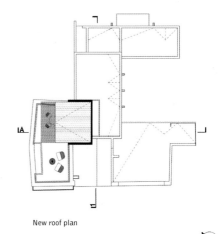

New roof plan

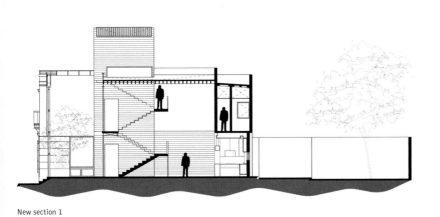

New section 1

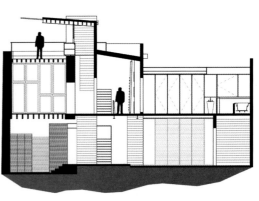

New section A

All living spaces are interconnected
to enhance visual continuity and open
to the outdoors wherever possible to
maximise a sense of space.

Alle Wohnbereiche sind miteinander
verbunden, um die visuelle Kontinuität
zu unterstreichen, und öffnen sich, wo
immer möglich, nach draußen, um das
Gefühl von Raum zu maximieren.

Tous les espaces à vivre sont
interconnectés pour accentuer la
continuité visuelle et ouvrir vers les
extérieurs aussi souvent que possible
pour optimiser le sentiment d'espace.

La continuidad visual se refuerza con
la conexión de todos los espacios de día.
Para maximizar la sensación de espacio,
estas estancias se abren al exterior en
la medida de sus posibilidades.

The staircase acts as a connector between the existing building and the new extension, whilst creating visual links and long sightlines.

Die Treppe dient als verbindendes Element zwischen dem bestehenden Gebäude und dem neuen Anbau und lässt gleichzeitig visuelle Verbindungen und lange Sichtachsen entstehen.

L'escalier fait la liaison entre les bâtiments existants et la nouvelle extension, tout en créant des liens visuels et de longues perspectives.

La escalera no solo es el vínculo entre el edificio original y la ampliación, sino que también genera lazos visuales y facilita las vistas dentro del interior de la casa.

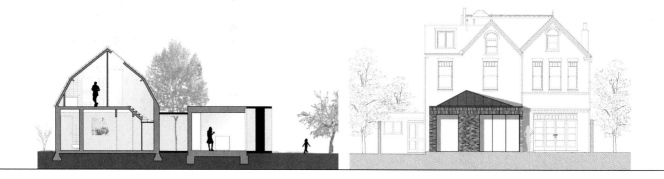

DIRECTORY

Adam Knibb Architects
Winchester, United Kingdom
www.adamknibbarchitects.com

AR Design Studio
Winchester, United Kingdom
http://ardesignstudio.co.uk

archicentre
Subang Jaya, Sengalor, Malaysia
www.archicentre.com.my

Ashton Porter Architects
London, United Kingdom
http://ashtonporter.com

Atelier Vens Vanbelle
Gent, Belgium
www.vensvanbelle.be

Buro Koek
s-Hertogenbosch, The Netherlands
www.burokoek.nl

Chris Dyson Architects
London, Bath; United Kingdom
www.chrisdyson.co.uk

Clear Architects
Loughton, Essex, United Kingdom
www.clear.gb.com

Clément Bacle architecte
Nantes, France
www.clementbaclearchitecte.fr

Exar Architecture
Brussels, Belgium
www.exar.be

FMD Architects
Melbourne, VIC, Australia
http://fmdarchitects.com.au

Henri Cleinge ARCHITECTE
Montreal, QC, Canada
www.cleinge.com

LABorstudio
Chihuahua, Mexico
Austin, TX, United States
www.laborstudio.com

LBMVarchitects
London, United Kingdom
www.lbmvarchitects.com

MARTIN FENLON ARCHITECTURE
Los Angeles, CA, United States
www.martinfenlon.com

Paper Igloo Architecture and Design
Kippen, Scotland, United Kingdom
www.paperigloo.com

Paul Archer Design
London, United Kingdom
www.paularcherdesign.co.uk

PROGETTOSPORE
Pistoia, PT, Italy
www.progettospore.org

Reset Architecture
's-Hertogenbosch, The Netherlands
www.resetarchitecture.com

Rever & Drage Architects
Flekkefjord, Oslo; Norway
www.reverdrage.no

RIACH architects
Oxford, United Kingdom
http://riacharchitects.com

Smart Design Studio
Surry hills, NSW, Australia
http://smartdesignstudio.com

Space Group of Architects
London, United Kingdom
www.spacegrouparchitects.com

Tigg + Coll Architects
London, United Kingdom
www.tiggcollarchitects.com

WY-TO architects
Paris, France
Singapore, Singapore
www.wy-to.com

Wyant Architecture
Philadelphia, Pennsylvania, United States
http://wyantarch.com

ZIEGLER Antonin architecte
Paris, France
http://antoninziegler.com